Also by Mike Winder

John R. Winder: Pioneer, Temple Builder, Dairyman

Counselors to the Prophets

The Christmas Animals
A children's book illustrated by Lindsey E. Ayres

Presiding Bishops

Utah in 2050: Glimpses of Our Future

Presidents and Prophets:
The Story of America's Presidents and the LDS Church

Life Lessons from Fathers of Faith:
Inspiring True Stories About Latter-day Dads
with Gary W. Toyn

When the White House Comes to Zion with Ronald L. Fox

It's Fun to Be the Mayor
A children's book illustrated by Andrea Vitali

Images of America: West Valley City

Called to Serve:
Celebrating Missionary Work around the World

Guy Stuff in the Scriptures

Favorite Scriptures of 100 American Leaders

HIDDEN IN HOLLYWOOD

The Gospel Found in 1001 Movie Quotes

Best wishes,

By Mike Winder

with Grace Winder, Research Assistant

2023
Eborn Books
Salt Lake City, Utah

ISBN: 9781609199074
Library of Congress Control Number: 2023945491

Eborn Books
1847 D Avenue
Tooele, Utah 84074
ebornbk@hotmail.com / www.ebornbooks.com

Printed in the United States of America
10 9 8 7 6 5 4 3 2 1

To Karyn, my favorite date for a movie!

CONTENTS

CONTENTS

CONTENTS

FOREWORD BY DOUG WRIGHT

I have always loved movies. As a kid growing up in Sugarhouse, my friends and I would often catch the downtown bus to the Uptown Theatre to see the latest Jerry Lewis movie or we'd score a ticket to the free Saturday morning kids flick at the Villa. When my friend Ross and I snuck off to see *Westside Story* at the Southeast Theatre my grandmother was not pleased, after all it was about hoodlums and violence!

My father was a projectionist at the old Woodland Drive-in and taught me to run 35mm arc lamp projectors when I was only twelve. That led to my being projectionist for the Wilford Ward's weekly movies and perhaps helped set the stage for my thirty-eight-year run hosting the *Movie Show* on KSL Radio. I was even the voice of *Nightmare Theatre* on Channel Four back in my Rock n Roll days at KCPX. I guess movies are just in my DNA.

Much of what is depicted on film is often criticized, and sadly, with good reason. I have walked out of screenings designed to give critics a preview of an upcoming feature. I've received some good-natured teasing about this but have also had support. My friend Sean Means at the *Salt Lake Tribune* actually ran a clock on me during a particularly dubious movie to see how long I'd last. In his published review he noted the minutes and seconds it took to drive me out but added, "God speed, Doug Wright!" I don't think he liked the movie either.

Hollywood can also leave me in awe. I love the films that put a lump in my throat, bring tears to my eyes and inspire me to do more and be more. That's why when Mike Winder contacted me and asked if I'd write this forward, I was happy to do so. It's so easy to focus on the bad and pick things apart, but to focus on the good and even search out the uplifting-well that takes a different skill set.

Over the years I've often quoted in speeches and even on-the-air, the very last line of the Thirteenth Article of Faith of The Church of Jesus Christ of Latter-Day Saints which states, "If there is anything lovely, virtuous or of good report we seek after these things." In this new book, *Hidden in Hollywood*, Mike has chosen to do exactly that; seek out the lovely, the virtuous and things of good report - in short, gospel principles to be found in cinema.

As I perused drafts of the book, I was impressed with the range of films that were included. There are topics and quotes from a myriad of genres; sci-fi, romance, thrillers, the classics, action films, Westerns and the list goes on. I was pleased to find quotes from my favorite John Wayne movie, *The Shootist,* and we even have Bill and Ted admonishing us to "Be excellent!" Although a compilation of wonderful quotes is certainly enjoyable and entertaining, it's the thoughtful commentary tying it all together with gospel insights that completes the book's purpose.

Motion pictures have often been described as "the art form of the Twentieth Century." Noted newspaper publisher, William Randolph Hearst said, "The coming of motion pictures was as important as that of the printing press." Josef Stalin saw film as "the greatest media of mass agitation." I believe that former first lady Eleanor Roosevelt got it just right when she said, "The film industry is a great industry, with infinite possibilities for good and bad. Its primary purpose is to entertain people. On the other side, it can do many other things. It can popularize certain ideals; it can make education palatable. But in the long run the judge who decides whether what it does is good or bad is the man or woman who attends the movies."

I'm pleased that *Hidden in Hollywood* has chosen to look at the good side in movies. After all, Yoda said, "When you look at the dark side careful you must be. For the dark side looks back."

Doug Wright
Salt Lake City, Utah
July 2023
Former host of KSL Radio's *The Movie Show*

INTRODUCTION

A few years ago, Greg Bennett at UtahValley360 had a fun blog quiz, "Who Said It: Prophet Or Princess?" Uplifting quotes were shared and the reader had to guess if the origin was from LDS General Conference or a Disney movie.[1] A couple months later, Matt Bennett at UtahValley360 had a similar post, "Who Said It: Dieter Or Dumbledore?" where quotes were shared from then-President Dieter F. Uchtdorf and the famous Hogwarts headmaster from the Harry Potter books and movies, Professor Albus Dumbledore. The reader had to guess who said what. "They both have silvery hair, speak with foreign accents and are known for their wisdom," Bennett said, and delightfully there were many matching themes.[2]

Both of these pieces were shared widely on social media and were a fun reminder that inspiration can indeed come from anywhere–including from movies! Those posts and my love of the movies inspired me to write this book.

No book can capture all of the gospel-related lines from the big screen (and some of the ones in this book are admittedly even a stretch), but a collection like this has never been made before.

---

[1] Greg Bennett, "Who Said It: Prophet Or Princess?" UtahValley360, 30 Jan 2014, online at https://utahvalley360.com/2014/01/30/who-said-it-princess-or-prophet/

[2] Matt Bennett, "Who Said It: Dieter Or Dumbledore?" UtahValley360, 1 Mar 2014, online at https://utahvalley360.com/2014/03/01/who-said-it-dieter-or-dumbledore/

For years, my teenage daughter Grace Winder and I have gathered over one-thousand movie quotes from well over 400 different films. Targeting a primarily LDS audience, this assemblage does not include quotes from R-rated movies. Just as enlightening to us as the movie quotes were the hundreds of quotes from church leaders and scriptures that matched up so well with these great movie quotes!

Even Brigham Young, while being around long before motion pictures, knew the power of creative performances to teach. "Upon the stage of a theater can be represented in character, evil and its consequences, good and its happy results and rewards; the weakness and the follies of man, the magnanimity of virtue and the greatness of truth," he said. "The stage [or the movie screen, I might add] can be made to aid the pulpit in impressing upon the minds of a community an enlightened sense of a virtuous life, also a proper horror of the enormity of sin and a just dread of its consequences."[3]

Back to Elder Uchtdorf. In recent years no latter-day leader has drawn life lessons to share from the movies like he has. "In a past general conference, I spoke about Bilbo Baggins—a very ordinary hobbit who sets out on an adventure to slay a dragon. Gandalf was his source of wisdom and help," he taught in 2021.

> "Or think of Obi-Wan Kenobi, who helps Luke Skywalker learn how to master the Force and defeat the Death Star. Anne of Green Gables has Marilla and Matthew, who love her and guide her as she goes from being an unwanted orphan to an accomplished student

---

[3] *Discourses of Brigham Young*, Selected by John A. Widtsoe, 1941, p. 243.

> and beloved friend. Hermione Granger and Harry Potter have caring teachers at Hogwarts School of Witchcraft and Wizardry to help them learn what they need to do to overcome 'He-Who-Must-Not-Be-Named.'

Elder Uchtdorf then said, "And now, I come to you. Whether you feel like a hero or not, you are one! You are the hero of your own life's story!"[4]

You are indeed the hero of your life's story, and the inspiring quotes from movies highlighted in this book can help you succeed on your real-life blockbuster adventure. So, if you are a movie fan, like I am, grab some popcorn and enjoy! You'll be amazed, and hopefully inspired, at the hundreds of gospel truths reinforced to us through the movies.

---

[4] Dieter F. Uchtdorf, "You Are the Hero of Your Own Story," *For the Strength of Youth,* February 2021.

I

LESSONS ON LIFE

The movies are packed with great, practical insights about life in general. Life is a gift, but it can be unpredictable and difficult. Life is an adventure that we should embrace with zeal, and yet everyone will script their own story. And ultimately, we must keep life in balance, because it is indeed precious and ultimately brief.

Life is a Gift

We've been taught our whole lives that our opportunity to be here on earth is a gift. Our life is a gift, has a plan, and has a purpose. The Primary kids even sing about it! Not only is life a gift, but as Elder Jeffrey R. Holland of the Quorum of the Twelve Apostles said, "Life is the most precious of all gifts."[1]

"People have forgotten what life is all about. They've forgotten what it is to be alive. They need to be reminded. They need to be reminded of what they have and what they can lose. What I feel is the joy of life, the gift of life, the freedom of life, the wonderment of life!"

–Robin Williams as Leonard Lowe in *Awakenings* (1990)

"I figure life is a gift and I don't intend on wasting it. You don't know what hand you're gonna get dealt next. You learn to take life as it comes at you . . . to make each day count."

–Leonardo DiCaprio as Jack Dawson in *Titanic* (1997)

---

[1] Jeffrey R. Holland, "Fear Not: Believe Only!" April 2022 General Conference.

"Look around, look around, at how lucky we are to be alive right now."

–Phillipa Soo as Eliza Schuyler in *Hamilton* (2020)

"Strange, isn't it? Each man's life touches so many other lives. When he isn't around he leaves an awful hole, doesn't he?"

–Henry Travers as Clarence Odbody in *It's a Wonderful Life* (1946)

"We just get the one life, you know. Just one. You can't live someone else's."

–Tia Leon as Gwen in *Ghost Town* (2008)

"Every day we have is one more than we deserve."

–Robert Redford as Warren Justice in *Up Close & Personal* (1996)

"I will never stop fighting for this life."

–Antonio Banderas as Puss in Boots in *Puss in Boots: The Last Wish* (2022)

Life is Unpredictable

Lucifer's plan for life was safe and predictable–we would all be forced to obey, we would all make it back to heaven, and, of course, the glory would be his. The Father's plan in contrast involved agency, which consequently made life both scary and wonderful, thanks to its unpredictability. "How interesting and unpredictable is the course of life,"[2] Elder Richard G. Hinckley of the Seventy once observed. Human behavior contributes to life's unpredictability. "For the ways of man are before the eyes of the Lord, and he pondereth all his goings," we read in Proverbs.[3]

"Who knows the ways of men?"

–Josh Gad as Olaf in *Frozen 2* (2019)

"Sometimes, I just don't understand human behavior."

–Anthony Daniels as C-3PO in *Star Wars: Episode V - The Empire Strikes Back* (1980)

"The only thing predictable about life is its unpredictability."

–Patton Oswalt as Remy in *Ratatouille* (2007)

"My mama always said, life was like a box of chocolates. You never know what you're gonna get."

–Tom Hanks as Forrest Gump in *Forrest Gump* (1994)

"I love waking up in the morning not knowing what's gonna happen or, who I'm gonna meet, where I'm gonna wind up."

–Leonardo DiCaprio as Jack Dawson in *Titanic* (1997)

---

[2] Richard G. Hinckley, "Prophetic Priorities," *BYU Speeches*, 15 May 2007.
[3] Proverbs 5:21

Larry Daley: "I have no idea what I'm going to do tomorrow."
Teddy Roosevelt: "How exciting!"

–Ben Stiller a Larry Daley and Robin Williams as Teddy Roosevelt in *Night at the Museum: Secret of the Tomb* (2014)

"Fasten your seatbelts, it's going to be a bumpy ride."

–Bette Davis as Margo in *All About Eve* (1950)

Life is Hard

This unpredictability can make life difficult. However, facing head-on the challenges of life are indeed what makes it great. "Looking back, I learned some of the best lessons during the hardest times—whether as a youth, on a mission, starting a new career, striving to magnify my callings, raising a large family, or struggling to be self-reliant," said Elder Stanley G. Ellis of the Seventy. "It seems clear that hard is good! Hard makes us stronger, humbles us, and gives us a chance to prove ourselves."[4]

"It's supposed to be hard. If it wasn't hard, everyone would do it. The hard is what makes it great."

–Tom Hanks as Jimmy Dugan in *A League of Their Own* (1992)

---

[4] Stanley G. Ellis, "Do We Trust Him? Hard Is Good," October 2017 General Conference.

"Life is hard. It's even harder when you're stupid."

–John Wayne as John Bernard Books in *The Shootist* (1976)

"Dying is easy, young man, living is harder."

–Christopher Jackson as George Washington in *Hamilton* (2020)

"Know that you're going to be tested every step of the way."

–Oprah Winfrey as Mrs. Which in *A Wrinkle in Time* (2018)

"Life tests you! Every day it brings you new chances for triumph or defeat."

–Liam Neeson as Qui-Gon Jinn in *Star Wars: Episode I - The Phantom Menace* (1999)

Life is an Adventure

Both the gospel and the movies remind us that life is an adventure. "You pass through the adventure of mortality only once," said Elder Uchtdorf to a worldwide audience of young adults. "Because God has given you your agency, you can choose many directions to go and still lead a fulfilling life. Mortality is an open-ended, choose-your-own-adventure story."[5] The ability to chart our own course, exercise our agency, and see what life has in store for us is a thrill that can persuade every heart.

---

[5] Dieter F. Uchtdorf, "Your Adventure through Mortality," *Ensign,* March 2019.

"To live... to live would be an awfully big adventure."
–Robin Williams as Peter Banning in *Hook* (1991)

"Adventure is out there!"
–Christopher Plummer as Charles Muntz in *Up* (2009)

"Every adventure requires a first step."
–Kathryn Beaumont as Alice in *Alice in Wonderland* (1951)

"There's the whole world at your feet."
–Dick Van Dyke as Bert in *Mary Poppins* (1964)

"There's a great big hunk of world down there with no fence around it."
–Larry Roberts as Tramp in *Lady and the Tramp* (1955)

"I'm going on an adventure!"[6]
–Martin Freeman as Bilbo Baggins in *The Hobbit: An Unexpected Journey* (2012)

---

[6] "The call to adventure has reached deep into his heart," Elder Uchtdorf said of Bilbo. "And so, this unremarkable hobbit leaves comfort behind and enters the path to a great adventure that will take him all the way to 'there and back again.'" Dieter F. Uchtdorf, "Your Great Adventure," October 2019 General Conference.

"I miss the desert. I miss the sea. And I miss waking up every morning wondering what wonderful adventure the new day will bring to us."

–John Rhys-Davies as Sallah in *Indiana Jones and the Dial of Destiny* (2023)

Live Life with Gusto

You have such great potential and promise in life that you should embrace it with delight. Having the gospel light to fill it with hope and joy gives us the confidence to go full speed ahead, knowing that everything will work out in the end and that Christ will make up the difference of any shortcomings along the way. I always loved the contagious enthusiasm for life preached by President Gordon B. Hinckley. "Love life and face its challenges and adversities as well as drink deeply of its enriching experiences and beauties," he said.[7] In other words, make life an occasion.

"Life's a garden: dig it."

–David Spade as Joe Dirt in *Joe Dirt* (2001)

Jerry: "So what do you think you'll do? How are you gonna spend your life?"
Joe: "I'm not sure. But I do know... I'm going to live every minute of it."

–Alice Braga as Jerry and Jamie Foxx as Joe in *Soul* (2020)

[7] Gordon B. Hinckley, "Rise to the Stature of the Divine within You," October 1989 General Conference.

"Live long and prosper."
–Leonard Nimoy as Spock in *Star Trek III: The Search for Spock* (1984)

"Your life is an occasion. Rise to it."
–Dustin Hoffman as Edward Magorium in *Mr. Magorium's Wonder Emporium* (2007)

"Life is good! But it can be better."
–Pedro Pascal as Max Lord in *Wonder Woman 1984* (2020)

"Life is a banquet and most poor suckers are starving to death!"
–Rosalind Russell as Mame Dennis in *Auntie Mame* (1958)

"Feel the rhythm! Feel the rhyme! Get on up, it's bobsled time!"
–Doug E. Doug as Sanka in *Cool Runnings* (1993)

Life is Different Paths

Since life is a "choose-your-own-adventure story," as Elder Uchtdorf put it earlier, everybody is going to have a different path. We should not be ashamed to take a path different from the world–the covenant path that follows the Savior. We can be like the ancient apostle Paul, who said, "I am not ashamed of the gospel of Christ: for it is the power of God unto salvation to every one that believeth."[8] And it is our focus that puts us on this path. "The development of character comes only as we focus on who we really are," said President Russell M. Nelson.[9]

"There's no shame in having a different path."

–Jimmy Smits as Kevin Rosario in *In the Heights* (2021)

"Whatever path you decide to take in this life...be true to yourself."

–Michelle Yeoh as Yu Shu Lien in *Crouching Tiger, Hidden Dragon* (2000)

"Life is full of possibilities. You just need to know where to look. Don't miss out on the joys of life."

–Jamie Foxx as Joe in *Soul* (2020)

"Always remember, your focus determines your reality."

–Liam Neeson as Qui-Gon Jinn in *Star Wars: Episode I - The Phantom Menace* (1999)

"My mama always said you can tell a lot about a person by their shoes, where they going, where they been."

–Tom Hanks as Forrest Gump in *Forrest Gump* (1994)

---

[8] Romans 1:16

[9] Russell M. Nelson, "Living by Scriptural Guidance," October 2000 General Conference.

Keep Life in Balance

Life is best when kept in balance. "The ride through mortality can be smoother for us when we strive to stay in balance," taught Elder M. Russell Ballard of the Twelve.[10] A great message on keeping life in balance was once shared by Elder W. Craig Zwick of the Seventy, where he referenced a popular movie. "The Lion King is a classic animated film about the African savanna," he began. "The lion prince reclaims the kingdom through the help of a mentor. His eyes are opened to the necessity of balance in the great circle of life on the savanna."[11]

"Everything you see exists together in a delicate balance. We are all connected in the great circle of life."

–James Earl Jones as Mufasa in *The Lion King* (1994)

"Lesson not just karate only. Lesson for whole life! Whole life have a balance, everything be better."

–Pat Morita as Mr. Miyagi in *The Karate Kid* (1984)

"Never be in a hurry. You'll miss the best parts in life."

–Marlene Dietrich as Saloon Hostess in *Around the World in 80 Days* (1956)

---

[10] M. Russell Ballard, "Keeping Life's Demands in Balance," April 1987 General Conference.

[11] Craig W. Zwick, "Lord, Wilt Thou Cause That My Eyes May Be Opened," October 2017 General Conference.

"When you feel life out of focus, always return to basic of life."
–Pat Morita as Mr. Miyagi in *The Karate Kid II* (1986)

Life is Short

As we get older, the years seem to accelerate. We watch loved ones pass away far too soon. We quickly figure out that life is indeed short. "The days of our probation are numbered, but none of us knows the number of those days," said Elder Joseph B. Wirthlin of the Twelve. "Each day of preparation is precious."[12] In the Book of Mormon, Amulek put it this way: "this life is the time for men to prepare to meet God; yea, behold the day of this life is the day for men to perform their labors."[13]

"Because in the end, none of us have very long on this Earth. Life is fleeting, so make your life spectacular."
–Robin Williams as Jack Powell in *Jack* (1996)

"I suppose in the end, the whole of life becomes an act of letting go."
–Irrfan Khan as Pi Patel in *Life of Pi* (2012)

---

[12] Joseph B. Wirthlin, "The Time to Prepare," April 1998 General Conference.
[13] Alma 34:32

"Life is short, forgive quickly, kiss slowly, love truly, laugh uncontrollably, and never regret anything that made you smile."

–Ryan Gosling as Noah Calhoun in *The Notebook* (2004)

"Death is what gives life meaning. To know your days are numbered. Your time is short."

–Tilda Swinton as The Ancient One in *Doctor Strange* (2016)

"Fear of death is what keeps us alive."

–Karl Urban as Dr. "Bones" McCoy in *Star Trek Beyond* (2016)

"Someone once told me that time was a predator that stalked us all our lives, but I rather believe that time is a companion who goes with us on the journey, and reminds us to cherish every moment because they'll never come again. What we leave behind is not as important as how we lived. After all, Number One, we're only mortal."

–Patrick Stewart as Jean Luc Picard in *Star Trek: Generations* (1994)

"How very special are we for just a moment to be part of life's eternal rhyme."

–Debbie Reynolds as Charlotte in *Charlotte's Web* (1973)

"It's not the years, honey. It's the mileage."

–Harrison Ford as Indiana Jones in *Raiders of the Lost Ark* (1981

2

DEATH & BEYOND

One of the great questions in life is how to make sense of death. Why do we die? What happens to us when we do? Where are our loved ones who have passed? The answers to questions like this are part of the peace the gospel brings. There are also dozens of movie quotes that help us better understand this doctrine.

Part of Life

The teachings of the restored gospel have been clear about the imperative role in our eternal progression that death plays. "Death is part of life. It is true," President Nelson taught. "We live to die, and we die to live again."[1] It would be unnatural for our time in mortality to last forever. Prophets and actors alike encourage us to be ready for when that day comes. "May we live so that when that final summons is heard, we may have no serious regrets, no unfinished business," encouraged President Thomas S. Monson.[2]

"It's all right, children. Life is made up of meetings and partings. That is the way of it."

–Steve Whitmire as Kermit the Frog as Bob Cratchit in *The Muppet Christmas Carol* (1992)

"Death is just a part of life, something we're all destined to do."

–Tom Hanks as Woody in *Toy Story 3* (2010)

---

[1] Russell M. Nelson, "Face the Future with Faith," April 2011 General Conference.

[2] Thomas S. Monson, "Now Is the Time," October 2001 General Conference.

"People die every day; friends, family. Harry may have died today, but he's still with us–in here (pointing to his heart)"

–Matthew Lewis as Neville Longbottom in *Harry Potter and the Deathly Hallows: Part 2* (2011)

"Turns out your friend here is only mostly dead. See, mostly dead is still slightly alive."

–Billy Crystal as Miracle Max in *The Princess Bride* (1987)[3]

"If you die trying for something important, then you have both honor and courage, and that's pretty good."

–Quinton Aaron as Michael Oher in *The Blind Side* (2009)

"Mama always said, dying was a part of life. I sure wish it wasn't."

–Tom Hanks as Forrest Gump in *Forrest Gump* (1994)

"Dust thou art, and unto dust shalt thou return."

–John Huston as God in *The Bible: In the Beginning . . .* (1966)

"I'm willing to die for what I believe. As should we all."

–Jennifer Lawrence as Katniss Everdeen in *The Hunger Games: Mockingjay - Part 1* (2014)

---

[3]See Alma 19:8 for a Book of Mormon example of this.

"We leave so many things unfinished in our lives."
–Malcolm McDowell as Dr. Soran in *Star Trek: Generations* (1994)

"Benjamin, we're meant to lose the people we love. How else would we know how important they are to us?"
–Edith Ivey as Mrs. Maple in *The Curious Case of Benjamin Button* (2008)

"You know, death is something many of us are uncomfortable speaking about. To die is human, and anything human is mentionable. Anything mentionable is manageable."
–Tom Hanks as Fred Rogers in *A Beautiful Day in the Neighborhood* (2019)

"Wilbur -- we're born, we live, and when our time comes, we die. It's just a natural cycle of life."
–Julia Robertson as Charlotte in *Charlotte's Web* (2006)

"The world keeps spinning, and the tables keep turning, and people come and go, but they're never forgotten."
–Salma Hayek as La Muerte in *The Book of Life* (2014)

Anticipating Death

It is natural to mourn those who die. "Thou shalt live together in love," we read in the Doctrine and Covenants, "insomuch that thou shalt weep for the loss of them that die."[4] Most people fear the Grim Reaper and the timing of their own death, too.

President Monson taught us why people fear death. "To most, there is something sinister and mysterious about this unwelcome visitor called death," he said. "Perhaps it is a fear of the unknown which causes many to dread its coming."[5] The gospel of Jesus Christ can give our hearts peace when we look towards death. We know it is part of a plan, and we know some things about what awaits us beyond the grave. The gospel plan can help reduce our fears about death. Afterall, greater than a fear of heights, spiders, or even public speaking is a widespread fear of death! Even the tough guys fear their light going out.

"Do you guys ever think about dying?"

–Margot Robbie as Barbie in *Barbie* (2023)

"I'm a dying man, scared of the dark."

–John Wayne as John Bernard Books in *The Shootist* (1976)

"We are food for worms, lads. Because, believe it or not, each and every one of us in this room is one day going to stop breathing, turn cold and die."

–Robin Williams as John Keating in *Dead Poets Society* (1989)

---

[4] D&C 42:45

[5] Thomas S. Monson, "Mrs. Patton—the Story Continues," October 2007 General Conference.

"It is the unknown we fear when we look upon death and darkness, nothing more."

–Michael Gambon as Albus Dumbledore in *Harry Potter and the Half-Blood Prince* (2009)

"Sorry, Pooh, but all stories have an ending, you know."

–Sebastian Cabot as the Narrator in *The Many Adventures of Winnie the Pooh* (1997)

"Part of the journey is the end."

–Robert Downey Jr. as Tony Stark in *Avengers: Endgame* (2019)

"Go in peace! I will not say 'do not weep,' for not all tears are an evil."

–Ian McKellen as Gandalf in *The Lord of the Rings: The Return of the King* (2013)

"To the well-organized mind, death is but the next great adventure."

–Richard Harris as Albus Dumbledore in *Harry Potter and the Sorcerer's Stone* (2001)

"I'm not afraid of death. I'm an old physicist - I'm afraid of time."

–Michael Caine as Dr. Brand in *Interstellar* (2014)

"Death is just nature's way of telling you to slow down."

–Walter Matthau as Morris Buttermaker in *The Bad News Bears* (1976)

"Old age. It's the only disease that you don't look forward to being cured of."

–Everett Sloan as Mr. Bernstein in *Citizen Kane* (1941)

"Dying is the day worth living for!"

–Geoffrey Rush as Barbossa in *Pirates of the Caribbean: At World's End* (2007)

"I'm not afraid to die. Although, it wouldn't be my first choice."

–Mark Rylance as Rudolf Abel in *Bridge of Spies* (2015)

"I've lived all five of my acts, and I am not asking you to be happy that I must go. I'm only asking that you turn the page, continue reading, and let the next story begin."

–Dustin Hoffman as Edward Magorium in *Mr. Magorium's Wonder Emporium* (2007)

"Death isn't sad. The sad thing is: most people don't live at all."

–Nick Nolte as Socrates in *Peaceful Warrior* (2006)

Moment of Death

In the plan of salvation, the day of death is a milestone, a graduation day, a day of new birth. "Death is a necessary component of our eternal existence. No one knows when it will come, but it is essential to God's great plan of happiness," taught President Nelson. "If we are well prepared, death brings no terror. From an eternal perspective, death is premature only for those who are not prepared to meet God," he said.[6]

Alma the Younger taught his sons, "the spirits of all men, whether they be good or evil, are taken home to that God who gave them life."[7] While sad for loved ones left behind, we are taught that it will be a glorious reunion for us when we pass onward. Returning home to God, as Alma taught, will be a wonderful rest from our earthly pains and the limitations of our physical bodies. President Monson once poetically called the edge of mortality the "threshold of infinity."[8]

"To infinity…and beyond!"
–Tim Allen as Buzz Lightyear in *Toy Story* (1995)

"I have no plans to die today."
–Chris Hemsworth as Thor in *Thor* (2011)

"You guys, this is exactly how I pictured my death!"
–Kate McKinnon as Jillian Holtzmann in *Ghostbusters* (2016)

"Death does not wait for you to be ready! Death is not considerate, or fair!"
–Ken Watanabe as Ra's al Ghul in *Batman Begins* (2005)

---

[6] Russell M. Nelson, "Now Is the Time to Prepare," April 2005 General Conference.
[7] Alma 40:11
[8] Thomas S. Monson, "He Is Risen!" April 2010 General Conference.

"All major changes are like death. You can't see what is on the other side until you get there."

–Jeff Goldblum as Dr. Ian Malcolm in *Jurassic Park* (1993)

After being asked what death feels like, "Quicker than falling asleep."

–Gary Oldman as Sirius Black in *Harry Potter and the Deathly Hallows: Part 2* (2011)

"I fell asleep without realizing it. And when I awakened, there were all my relatives speaking in low tones and saying nothing but the kindest things about me. Then I knew I was dead."

–Don Ameche as Henry Van Cleve in *Heaven Can Wait* (1943)

After being asked what it is like to die, "Like... being born, only backwards."

–Malachi Pearson as Casper the Friendly Ghost in *Casper* (1995)

"A good death is its own reward."

–Antje Traue as Faora in *Man of Steel* (2013)

"Souls don't die."

–Vin Diesel as the Iron Giant in *The Iron Giant* (1999)

Death is Not the End

As we pass through the veil and into the bright light of heaven, we will realize that death is not the end and that we are who we have always truly been–just now without our body once more. In fact, we are in the spirit world. And this world will be a better one. Moroni taught, “Whoso believeth in God might with surety hope for a better world, yea, even a place at the right hand of God.”[9] We know that our character will exist in the spirit world while our riches surely will not. We know that our personal identity will continue and that “Whatever principle of intelligence we attain unto in this life, it will rise with us in the resurrection.”[10] This destiny is taught by Sunday school teachers here on earth and by both superheroes and wizards in the movies.

"End? No, the journey doesn't end here. Death is just another path. One that we all must take.”

–Ian McKellen as Gandalf in *The Lord of the Rings: The Return of the King* (2013)

“In my culture, death is not the end. It's more of a stepping off point.”

–Chadwick Boseman as the Black Panther in *Captain America: Civil War* (2016)

“Light bulbs die, my sweet. I will depart.”

–Dustin Hoffman as Edward Magorium in *Mr. Magorium's Wonder Emporium* (2007)

---

[9] Ether 12:4

[10] D&C 130:18

Charly: "It's not the end."
Sam: "What if I was wrong? What if there's nothing after this and it's all just a lie?"
Charly: "It doesn't feel like a lie."

–Heather Beers as Charlene 'Charly' Riley and Jeremy Hoop as Sam Roberts in *Charly* (2002)

"Imagine what he is seeing up there, just imagine!"

–Cloris Leachman as Memaw in *I Can Only Imagine* (2018)

"A whole new world–a new fantastic point of view."

–Scott Weinger as Aladdin in *Aladdin* (1992)

"There is a happy land, far far away, where saints in glory stand bright, bright as day!"

–Terry Saunders as Lady Thiang in *The King and I* (1956)

"Roads? Where we're going, we don't need roads."

–Christopher Lloyd as Dr. Emmett Brown in *Back to the Future* (1985)

"Circumstances have taught me that a man's ethics are the only possessions he will take beyond the grave."

–Morgan Freeman as Hibble in *Moll Flanders* (1996)

"Nothing is gone forever, only out of place."
–Emily Blunt as Mary Poppins in *Mary Poppins Returns* (2018)

"A place where we all go can't be bad, can it girl?"
–Robin Williams as Dr. Chris Nielsen in *What Dreams May Come* (1998)

Departed Still with Us

In the hereafter, we will still care for our loved ones left behind here in mortality. "Sometimes the veil between this life and the life beyond becomes very thin," said President Ezra Taft Benson. "Our loved ones who have passed on are not far from us," he said.[11] President Joseph F. Smith also spoke of our deceased family and friends. "We are not separate from them," he said. "We live in their presence, they see us, they are solicitous for our welfare, they love us now more than ever."[12] We know from latter-day teachings that the dead still care for us and feel that they have a work to do to help our families be strong for the eternities. Not only do the hearts of the children still alive turn to their deceased fathers, but an omnipotent Heavenly Father "shall turn the heart of the fathers to the children."[13]

[11] Ezra Taft Benson, "Life Is Eternal," April 1971 General Conference.
[12] Joseph F. Smith, *Conference Report,* April 1916, 2–3.
[13] Malachi 4:6

To his daughter Pocahontas about her late mother, "She is still with us. Whenever the wind moves through the trees, I feel her presence."

–Russell Means as Chief Powhatan in *Pocahontas* (1995)

"The most important thing is, even if we're apart, I'll always be with you."

–Brady Bluhm as Christopher Robin in *Pooh's Grand Adventure: The Search for Christopher Robin* (1997)

When Harry Potter asked why his deceased loved ones were near, "We never left."

–Geraldine Somerville as Lily Potter in *Harry Potter and the Deathly Hallows: Part 2* (2011)

"Sometimes the spirit gets yanked out so fast that the essence still feels it has work to do here."

–Whoopi Goldberg as Oda Mae Brown in *Ghost* (1990)

"The dead don't die. They look on and help."

–Samantha Morton as Agatha in *Minority Report* (2002)

"The great kings of the past look down on us from those stars."

–James Earl Jones as Mufasa in *The Lion King* (1994)

"You think the dead we loved truly ever leave us? You think that we don't recall them more clearly in times of great trouble?"

–Michael Gambon as Albus Dumbledore in *Harry Potter and the Prisoner of Azkaban* (2004)

"A man tells his stories so many times that he becomes the stories. They live on after him, and in that way he becomes immortal."

–Billy Crudup as Will Bloom in *Big Fish* (2003)

"Your mother's gone. But what she stood for, what she fought for... that's not gone."

–Harrison Ford as Han Solo in *Star Wars: Episode IX - The Rise of Skywalker* (2019)

"Trust she's always there, watching as you grow. Find her in the place where the lost things go."

–Emily Blunt as Mary Poppins in *Mary Poppins Returns* (2018)

"No one's ever really gone."

–Mark Hamill as Luke Skywalker in *Star Wars: Episode VIII - The Last Jedi* (2017)

Conquering Death

We believe that time is different in the eternities and that families can be together forever someday. Because of Jesus of Nazareth, the literal Son of God rising again, the resurrection will be a reality for all of us. He is our Savior and Redeemer. What joy this gives all of us who have lost friends and family and who are anxious about our own mortality! “We live to die,” said President Nelson, “and we die to live again.”[14] Having a better grasp on what really happens when we die, as taught by the gospel and sometimes put into words in movies, we learn that death need not be as feared as it often is.

“The Messiah has come! A man was dead but now he lives!”
–Van Heflin as Bar Amand in *The Greatest Story Ever Told* (1965)

“I just feel as if I’ve been asleep for a long time and now suddenly I’m awake.”
–Amy Adams as Amelia Earhart in *Night at the Museum: Battle of the Smithsonian* (2009)

“A whole human life is just a heartbeat here in Heaven. Then we'll all be together forever.”
–Robin Williams as Chris Nielsen in *What Dreams May Come* (1998)

“Death cannot stop true love. All it can do is delay it for a while.”
–Cary Elwes as Westley in *The Princess Bride* (1987)

---

[14] Russell M. Nelson, “Face the Future with Faith,” April 2011 General Conference.

Ultimately, the third brother in the story about the Deathly Hallows "greeted Death as an old friend and went with him gladly, departing this life as equals."

–Emma Watson as Hermione Granger in *Harry Potter and the Deathly Hallows: Part 1* (2010)

"After all, you know there are worse things in life than death."

–Woody Allen as Boris Grushenko in *Love and Death* (1975)

3

LEAPS OF FAITH

Faith, as every saint knows, is the first principle of the gospel. It is the first step needed in our walk back to our heavenly home. Faith may be the first small step towards exaltation, but it is a powerful one. "If ye have faith," the Master taught his disciples, "nothing shall be impossible unto you."[1] Fortunately, the movies have plenty to say about faith.

Faith and Sight

What is faith? The word is rattled around the Sunday schools so often it is worth pausing to better understand what it is. Hollywood often connects faith with sight. "Faith is the substance of things hoped for," Paul wrote to the Hebrews, "the evidence of things not seen."[2] Not only can seeing things with our hearts be insightful, but at times it may be even more accurate than trusting our natural eyes. "Hope helps us to walk by faith, not by sight. This can actually be safer," explained the late apostle Elder Neal A. Maxwell. "When unaided spiritually, natural sight often shrinks from the odds," he said.[3] Illusions can easily deceive the eyes, but the spirit confirming our faith is real. "For we walk by faith, not by sight," Paul wrote to those in Corinth.[4]

"Faith, Andy, is the belief in something for which we have no evidence."

–Jason Robards as Charles Wheeler in *Philadelphia* (1993)

---

[1] Matthew 17:20
[2] Hebrews 11:1
[3] Neal A. Maxwell, "Brightness of Hope," October 1994 General Conference.
[4] 2 Corinthians 5:7

"Faith is believing when common sense tells you not to."

–John Payne as Fred Gailey in *Miracle on 34th Street* (1947)

"There may be something there that wasn't there before."

–Angela Lansbury as Mrs. Potts in *Beauty and the Beast* (1991)

"Your eyes can deceive you, don't trust them."

–Alec Guinness as Obi-Wan Kenobi in *Star Wars: Episode IV - A New Hope* (1977)

"Seeing isn't believing; believing is seeing."

–Eric Lloyd as Charlie Calvin in *The Santa Clause 2* (2002)

Faith in Others and Faith in God

It is good to have faith in others and to believe in yourself. "Believe in yourself and then live so as to reach your possibilities," President Monson once said.[5] Apostle Marvin J. Ashton pointed out, "Successful people have this in common—they have faith in others."[6] But there is something even greater than having faith in mere mortals, and that is faith in the Higher Power that perfectly loves us all. It is faith in God the Father and His Son Jesus Christ that is the vital principle of the gospel. It is faith in the Father's plan and faith in our Redeemer's role in

---

[5] Thomas S. Monson, "Living the Abundant Life," *Liahona,* January 2012.

[6] Marvin J. Ashton, "Friends to Prisoners and Prophets" *Ensign,* July 1986.

it that will set us on the path to returning home. What do you believe? Who do you have faith in?

"It's time to ask yourself what you believe."

–Julian Glover as Walter Donovan in *Indiana Jones and the Last Crusade* (1989)

"My faith's in people, I guess. Individuals. And I'm happy to say that, for the most part, they haven't let me down."

–Chris Evans as Steve Rogers in *Captain America: Civil War* (2016)

"Have a little faith in people."

–Owen Wilson as Jack Ryan in *The Big Bounce* (2004)

"You must always have faith in people, and, most importantly, you must always have faith in yourself."

–Reese Witherspoon as Elle Woods in *Legally Blonde* (2001)

"In a world full of people afraid to believe in anything, it was your wide-eyed, obstinate, happily-ever-after faith – in life, in God, and in me."

–Heather Beers as Charlene 'Charly' Riley in *Charly* (2002)

"We cannot be lost as long as we keep faith in God and in ourselves."

–Gérard Depardieu as Christopher Columbus in *1492: Conquest of Paradise* (1992)

"God tells us, true faith is the freedom to choose truth."
–Nicholas Farrell as Robert in *Driving Lessons* (2006)

"The only thing that matters is what you believe. History shows us Jesus was an extraordinary man. A human inspiration. That's it. That's all the evidence has ever proved. But, when I was a boy–when I was down in that well Teabing told you about–I thought I was going to die, Sophie. And what I did, I prayed. I prayed to Jesus to keep me alive so I could see my parents again, so I could go to school again, so I could play with my dog. Sometimes I wonder if I wasn't alone down there."
–Tom Hanks as Robert Langdon in *The DaVinci Code* (2006)

"Just because you can't see something, it doesn't mean it's not there."
–Kaya Scodelario as Carina Smyth Barbossa in *Pirates of the Caribbean: Dead Men Tell No Tale*s (2017)

"Just because you can't see the air doesn't keep you from breathing. And just because you can't see God doesn't keep you from believing."
–Justin Pierre Edmund as Jeremiah Biggs in *The Preacher's Wife* (1996)

Developing Faith

Even though we all must develop faith in the Lord Jesus Christ, this comes easier for some than others. When faith comes naturally to some this should be appreciated as the spiritual gift that it is. "If you cannot say you know God is there, you can hope that He is," encouraged President Uchtdorf. "You can desire to believe," he said. "That is enough to start."[7] Most of us have to work to develop our faith. Alma taught the Zoramites that faith is like a seed that is planted in our hearts. "If ye do not cast it out by your unbelief, that ye will resist the Spirit of the Lord, behold, it will begin to swell within your breasts."[8] Mr. Miyagi and others taught similar facts in our favorite films.

"Inside you have strong root. No need nothing except what inside you to grow."

–Pat Morita as Mr. Miyagi in *The Karate Kid* (1984)

"Faith is a gift which I have yet to receive."

–Tom Hanks as Robert Langdon in *Angels and Demons* (2009)

"To find something, anything, a great truth or a lost pair of glasses, you must first believe there would be some advantage in finding it."

–Jude Law as Jack Burden in *All the King's Men* (2006)

---

[7] Dieter F. Uchtdorf, "He Will Place You on His Shoulders and Carry You Home," April 2016 General Conference.

[8] Alma 32:28

"You must believe, boy. You must believe."

–Sean Connery as Dr. Henry Jones in *Indiana Jones and the Last Crusade* (1989)

"When you believe in a thing, believe in it all the way, implicitly and unquestionable."

–Frank Morgan as The Wizard of Oz in *The Wizard of Oz* (1939)

Edward: "I envy people who have faith, I just can't get my head around it."
Carter: "Maybe because your head's in the way."

–Jack Nicholson as Edward Perriman Cole and Morgan Freeman as Carter Chambers in *The Bucket List* (2007)

"I want to compare faith to running in a race. It's hard. It requires concentration of will, energy of soul."

–Ian Charleson as Eric Liddell in *Chariots of Fire* (1981)

"If you focus on what you've left behind, you will never be able to see what lies ahead!"

–Brad Garrett as Chef Gusteau in *Ratatouille* (2007)

"I've come to believe it's not so much about what you believe, it's how hard you believe it."

–Harrison Ford as Indiana Jones in *Indiana Jones and the Dial of Destiny* (2023)

Faith and Works

We can put our faith to the test by acting on it, for faith without works is dead, as James taught, and we are better to show our faith with our works.[9] We see the hand of God best when we act on our faith. "Dispute not because ye see not," admonished Moroni, "for ye receive no witness until after the trial of your faith."[10] The movies show that faith is wonderful, but we must always do our part, demonstrating our belief with action. For example, the nuns in the *Sound of Music* removed the distributor wires so that the Nazis' car wouldn't start, helping to answer their own prayers that Maria and the Von Trapp family would successfully escape.

"I have faith, I just need proof to back it up."

–Joseph Mazzello as Joe Wenteworth in *Simon Burch* (1998)

"Nothing is impossible as long as you carry with you a little bit of faith and a big roll of electrical tape."

–Kathy Najimy as Sister Mary Patrick in *Sister Act 2: Back in the Habit* (1993)

"If you build it, he will come."

–Lee Garlington as The Voice in *Field of Dreams* (1989)[11]

---

[9] James 2:17-18

[10] Ether 12:6

[11] "Let us, with faith unwavering and with love unstinting, be bridge builders to the hearts of those with whom we labor. As in the movie, *Field of Dreams*, if we build it, they will come." -Thomas S. Monson, "They Will Come," April 1997 General Conference.

"My faith protects me. My Kevlar helps."
–Gary Oldman as Jim Gordon in *The Dark Knight* (2008)

"Faith is my sword. Truth is my shield. Knowledge my armor."
–Benedict Cumberbatch as Dr. Stephen Strange in *Doctor Strange* (2016)

Faith to Accomplish Good

Faith is a powerful thing, and can be our secret weapon in achieving the impossible. "There is no obstacle too great, no challenge too difficult, that we cannot meet with faith," said President Hinckley.[12] Faith can help us achieve our potential, see the truth, and overcome obstacles. In our Father's plan of salvation, all of His children will receive their just degree of glory in the end and their faith will indeed be rewarded. Our faith becomes something very personal, something that nobody can take away. It always triumphs in the end when applied for accomplishing good.

"The only way to achieve the impossible is to believe the possible."
–Mia Wasikowska as Alice Kingsleig in *Alice Through the Looking Glass* (2016)

---

[12] Gordon B. Hinckley, "God Grant Us Faith," October 1983 General Conference.

"Everything is possible, even the impossible."

–Emily Blunt as Mary Poppins in *Mary Poppins Returns* (2018)

"Anything's possible Lawrence. If it can be dreamed, it can be done."

–Robin Williams as Teddy Roosevelt in *Night at the Museum* (2006)

"Odds against them didn't stop those men (Founding Fathers). They were fools that way. All the good that ever came into this world came from fools with faith like that."

–Jean Arthur as Clarissa Saunders in *Mr. Smith Goes to Washington* (1939)

"I've learned life is a lot like surfing. When you get caught in the impact zone, you need to get right back up. Because you never know what's over the next wave. And if you have faith, anything is possible, anything at all."

–AnnaSophia Robb as Bethany Hamilton in *Soul Surfer* (2011)

"Pharaoh has the power. He can take away your food, your home, your freedom. He can take away your sons and daughters. With one word, Pharaoh can take away your very lives. But there is one thing he cannot take away from you: your faith. Believe, for we will see God's wonders."

–Val Kilmer as Moses in *The Prince of Egypt* (1998)

"Sometimes the truth isn't good enough. Sometimes people deserve more. Sometimes people deserve to have their faith rewarded."

–Christian Bale as Bruce Wayne in *The Dark Knight* (2008)

"Don't you see, Hook? You will never win, not as long as there's faith, trust, and pixie dust."

–Harriet Owen as Jane in *Return to Neverland* (2002)

Taking the Leap of Faith

The philosophers and theologians have long called that step into the unseen world of belief a "leap of faith," and rightly so. Too often we want to see the end, and know clearly the answers of life's tests before we get too far. However, we "must learn to walk to the edge of the light, and then a few steps into the darkness;" as President Harold B. Lee put it; "then the light will appear and show the way before you."[13]

One of the best scenes from the movies showcasing this principle is in *Indiana Jones and the Last Crusade*, when our hero is going through the final traps and tests to get to the long sought after Holy Grail. Indy has to cross a large chasm and realizes that he must take a bold step into the void with the hope that something will support him when he does.

[13] Quoted in Boyd K. Packer, "The Edge of the Light," *BYU Magazine*, March 1991.

"It's a leap of faith."

–Harrison Ford as Indiana Jones in *Indiana Jones and the Last Crusade* (1989)

"Sometimes, you have to take a leap of faith first. The trust part comes later."

–Corburn Gross as Father Daniel Leone in *Man of Steel* (2013)

"Don't you want to take a leap of faith? Or become an old man, filled with regret."

–Ken Watanabe as Mr. Saito in *Inception* (2010)

"I just keep thinking of that C.S. Lewis line, 'Only a real risk can test the reality of a belief.'"

–Shane Harper as Josh Wheaton in *God's Not Dead* (2014)

"Love without faith, like religion without faith, doesn't amount to very much."

–Lawrence Grant as Reverend Mr. Carmichael in *Shanghai Express* (1932)

"We have nothing if not belief."

–Simon Pegg as Reepicheep in *The Chronicles of Narnia: The Voyage of the Dawn Treader* (2010)

"Some days, faith is all you need."

–Ben Affleck as Matt Murdock in *Daredevil* (2003)

"Faith makes things turn out right."

–Michelle Stacy as Penny in *The Rescuers* (1977)

"I find your lack of faith disturbing."

–James Earl Jones as Darth Vader in *Star Wars: Episode IV - A New Hope* (1977)

4

THE FATHER & THE SON

Joseph Smith taught "The first principle of truth and of the Gospel is to know for a certainty the character of God."[1] Remarkably, hidden in the movies are fun and insightful quotes that help us better understand our Heavenly Family, including both the Father and the Son.

Our Heavenly Family

God's Plan is family focused–and we are blessed to have both an earthly family and a Heavenly Family. We have not seen our Heavenly Father or Heavenly Mother with our mortal eyes, but they are there; eagerly waiting for us all to return home. "'Return with Honor,' can be applied to each of us on our eternal path of progression," reminded Elder Robert D. Hales of the Twelve.[2] Not only are we children of God, but He has sent us here. The joyful day of returning to Heavenly Father and Mother should be a torch of hope for each of us in this life.

"You are not alone on this journey," President Uchtdorf likewise said to us. "Your Heavenly Father knows you. Even when no one else hears you, He hears you," he taught.[3] Key to the eventual reuniting of our Heavenly Family is the help of an Elder Brother, who, as President Dallin H. Oaks taught, "gives each of us the opportunity to repent of our sins and return clean

---

[1] Joseph Fielding Smith, editor, *Teachings of the Prophet Joseph Smith*, p. 345.
[2] Robert D. Hales, "Return with Honor," *Ensign,* June 1999.
[3] Dieter F. Uchtdorf, "Your Wonderful Journey Home," April 2013 General Conference.

to our heavenly home."[4] We all have this potential to come home. In his final chapter, Nephi prayed that "many of us, if not all," would return to our Heavenly Home.[5]

"You have another family, far away, one you have never seen."
–Ian Holm as Capitaine Phillippe D'Arnot in *Greystoke: The Legend of Tarzan, Lord of the Apes* (1984)

"We are not just servants of God, we are His children, and we are all part of one heavenly family."
–Greg Kinnear as Todd Burpo in *Heaven Is for Real* (2014)

"Because of who you are, you are about to find your parents. And when you do that, you'll be home."
–Albert Brooks as Marlin in *Finding Dory* (2016)

"I won't let you down, father!"
–Tate Donavan as Hercules in *Hercules* (1997)

"You are not alone. Believe me. No one is alone."
–Anna Kendrick as Cinderella in *Into the Woods* (2014)

"Alone, never have you been."
–Frank Oz as Yoda in *Star Wars: Episode IX – The Rise of Skywalker* (2019)

---

[4] Dallin H. Oaks, "What Has Our Savior Done for Us?" April 2021 General Conference.
[5] 2 Nephi 33:12

"You feel like you're all alone here, but you're not!"
–Owen Wilson as Nate in *Wonder* (2017)

"Everybody comes home."
–Mark Ruffalo as Hulk in *Avengers: Endgame* (2019)

"I can sense you there, like a friend I've always known. Are you the one I've been looking for all of my life? Show yourself. I'm ready to learn."
–Idina Menzel as Elsa in *Frozen 2* (2019)

Creator of Heaven and Earth

To provide a mortal experience for all of His children, God created a remarkable blue planet for us to come to. It's a marvelous world in which to gain a body and learn lessons we could not elsewhere! God's artistry in creating knows no bounds. The prophet Alma would agree with several movie characters that point to the wonders of creation as proof of God's existence. "All things denote there is a God; yea, even the earth, and all things that are upon the face of it," he said; "yea, and its motion, yea, and also all the planets which move in their regular form do witness that there is a Supreme Creator."[6]

The Bible starts out with the story of the Creation. "In the beginning God created the heaven and the earth," begins

[6] Alma 30:44

Genesis.[7] Verses talk of a world originally immersed in water before it was separated from the dry land. Everything was created spiritually before it was created physically, and all was known and numbered unto Him. The Earth is good–from the soaring mountains, to the lush forests, from the lonely deserts, to the ocean depths. Among those creatures are men and women. God knows us, and knows our attributes. He created all, and on the seventh day, He rested.

"I'm the one. Creator of the heavens and the earth, Alpha and Omega."[8]

–Morgan Freeman as God in *Bruce Almighty* (2003)

To his friend Truman while enjoying a magical sunset: "That's the big guy. What a big paintbrush he's got."

–Noah Emmerich as Marlon in *The Truman Show* (1998)

"We paint with brushes, and He paints with a billion stars and a trillion galaxies."

–Britt Robertson as Melissa Henning in *I Still Believe* (2020)

"There's a huge universe out there. With a lot of galaxies."

–Anya Taylor-Joy as Princess Peach in *The Super Mario Bros. Movie* (2023)

---

[7] Genesis 1:1, 6

[8] See Revelations 1:8.

"How can you see places like this (looking into the star-filled sky) and have moments like this and not believe? In fact, there are some things that they call miraculous. Einstein said the more he studied the universe, the more he believed in a higher power."

–Mandy Moore as Jamie Sullivan in *A Walk to Remember* (2002)

"Thank the Maker!"

–Anthony Daniels as C-3PO in *Star Wars: Episode IV - A New Hope* (1977)

"In the beginning, there was only ocean."

–Rachel House as Gramma Tala in *Moana* (2016)

"I will make a man more precious than fine gold; even a man than the golden wedge of Ophir."

–John Huston as God in *The Bible: In the Beginning . . .* (1966)

"I know every rock and tree and creature has a life, has a spirit, has a name."

–Irene Bedard as Pocahontas in *Pocahontas* (1995)

"Buddy, I've been around the world many times when I was a young cumulus nimbus cloud. It's a wonderful place, filled with wondrous creatures."

–Leon Redbone as Leon the Snowman in *Elf* (2003)

"You have the ability to make people laugh. I know, I created you."

–Morgan Freeman as God in *Bruce Almighty* (2003)

"God made countries, God makes kings, and the rules by which they govern, and those rules say that the Sabbath is His. And I for one intend to keep it that way."

–Ian Charleson as Eric Liddell in *Chariots of Fire* (1981)

The Son of God

The premortal Jehovah, who led the creation, was sent to Earth as the son of a Divine Father and an earthly mother. With the heavenly attributes inherited from His Heavenly Father, the Son was a God walking among men. With the birth of Christ, the angels on Judea's plains heralded His birth, and joyous singing commemorating the Babe in Bethlehem has sounded forth for two millennia since. True Christians even in the movies know that Christmas is more about Jesus, music, and love than greed, gluttony, and commercialism. During his ministry, Jesus taught others to be kind to each other and keep the commandments.

But it was not merely His divine example, His miracles, or His teachings that set Jesus apart from all who have walked this earth. It was His willingness to suffer and die for all; a perfect man satisfying both justice and mercy through the Atonement of Jesus Christ. The self-sacrifice of Aslan the Lion in *The Lion the Witch and the Wardrobe* is a clear type of the Savior's gift.

Through the life and mission of Jesus Christ, our Savior has purchased all of our souls so that we can return to the marvelous light of God's presence. And this Jesus of Nazareth, now the Resurrected Christ, will return someday in all His glory. "While we are powerless to alter the fact of the Second Coming and unable to know its exact time," said President Oaks, "we can accelerate our own preparation."[9]

"Have you found Jesus yet, Gump?"

–Gary Sinise as Lt. Daniel Taylor in *Forrest Gump* (1994)

"He'll be a god to them."

–Russell Crowe as Jor-El in *Man of Steel* (2013)

"Remember upon Christmas Day who made lame beggars walk and blind men see."

–Jerry Nelson as Tiny Tim Cratchit in *The Muppet Christmas Carol* (1992)

Narrator: "Every Who down in Whoville, the tall and the small was singing without any presents at all."
The Grinch: "Maybe Christmas (he thought) doesn't come from a store. Maybe Christmas perhaps means a little bit more."

–Anthony Hopkins as Narrator and Jim Carrey as The Grinch in *How the Grinch Stole Christmas* (2000)

---

[9] Dallin H. Oaks, "Preparation for the Second Coming," April 2004 General Conference.

"The best way to spread Christmas cheer is singing loud for all to hear."

–Will Ferrell as Buddy the Elf in *Elf* (2003)

"Go now, and teach all nations. Make it your first care to love one another and to find the kingdom of God, and all things shall be yours without me asking,"

–Max von Sydow as Jesus of Nazareth in *The Greatest Story Ever Told* (1965)

"If you're going to follow in someone's footsteps, who better than Christ?"

–Owen Wilson as Kevin Rawley in *Meet the Parents* (2000)

"He has taken the world of our sins onto Himself. To this end He said He was born, in that stable, where I first saw Him. For this cause, He came into the world."[10]

–Finaly Currie as Balthasar in *Ben-Hur* (1959)

"But you must remember, Mowgli, greater love hath no one than he who lays down his life for his friend."

–Sebastian Cabot as Bagheera in *The Jungle Book* (1967)

"God has brought you out of darkness, I have bought your soul for God."

–Colm Wilkinson as the Bishop in *Les Misérables* (2012)

---

[10] See John 18:37.

"When a willing victim who has committed no treachery, is killed in a traitor's stead, the stone table will crack, and even death itself would turn backwards."

–Liam Neeson as Aslan in *Chronicles of Narnia: The Lion, the Witch and the Wardrobe* (2005)

"It is finished."[11]

–Liam Neeson as Aslan in *Chronicles of Narnia: The Lion, the Witch and the Wardrobe* (2005)

"The search for the Cup of Christ is the search for the divine in all of us."

–Denholm Elliott as Marcus Brody in *Indiana Jones and the Last Crusade* (1989)

"I think that you had better get up. I think that God is coming."

–Joseph Thiaka as Kamante in *Out of Africa* (1985)

How God Works

As His children, humanity has long looked into the heavens and wondered why God does what He does, and doesn't do what He doesn't do. But as Apostle D. Todd Christofferson reminded us, "We ought not to think of God's plan as a cosmic vending

[11] See John 19:30.

machine where we (1) select a desired blessing, (2) insert the required sum of good works, and (3) the order is promptly delivered."[12] Movies sometimes remind us that God is there, but that He answers us in His own way and with His own schedule. "Faith in God includes faith in God's timing," reminded Elder Maxwell.[13]

Therefore, we must take care to receive His counsel, and not to attempt to counsel the Lord. Gratefully, He does hear us and love us and–if we will listen–will guide us. If we do listen for Him, we can receive "the peace of God, which passeth all understanding."[14] Those who put their faith in God will also see opportunities come at His mercy. Numerous Hollywood films remind us that He opens windows when doors get shut and gives other hints at how God truly works in the affairs of His children.

"God works in mysterious ways, His wonders to perform."
–Loretta Young as Julia Brougham in *The Bishop's Wife* (1947)

"The ways of the Lord are not our ways. And what He hath intended or how it shall be perfected is not in our power to know. Only in the trust of what is to come can we prosper."
–George C. Scott as Abraham in *The Bible: In the Beginning...* (1966)

---

[12] D. Todd Christofferson, "Our Relationship with God," April 2022 General Conference.
[13] Neal A. Maxwell, "The Holy Ghost: Glorifying Christ," *Ensign*, July 2002.
[14] Philippians 4:7

"Sometimes God does things for reasons we don't understand, but someday everything will make perfect sense."

–Pete Coyote as Reverend Sullivan in *A Walk to Remember* (2002)

"If there is a higher power, why is it He can't get you a new sweater?"

–Clayne Crawford as Dean in *A Walk to Remember* (2002)

"The Kingdom of God is not a democracy. The Lord never seeks re-election. There are no referenda on which road to take. There's one right, one wrong, one absolute ruler."

–Ian Charleson as Eric Liddell in *Chariots of Fire* (1981)

"Maybe the real God uses tricks, you know? Maybe He's not omnipotent. He's just been around so long He knows everything."

–Bill Murray as Phil in *Groundhog Day* (1993)

<u>Chris:</u> "Where is God in all of this?"
<u>Albert:</u> "Oh, he's up there, somewhere shouting down that he loves us. Wondering why we can't hear him."

–Robin Williams as Chris Nielsen and Cuba Gooding, Jr. as Albert Lewis in *What Dreams May Come* (1998)

"Anything is possible when you have inner peace."

–Randall Duk Kim as Master Oogway in *Kung Fu Panda* (2008)

"By myself, I am nothing. It is the power of God which uses me to work His will."

–Charlton Heston as Moses in *The Ten Commandments* (1965)

"Son, in thirty-five years of religious study, I've come up with only two hard, incontrovertible facts; there is a God, and, I'm not Him."

–Robert Prosky as Father Cavanaugh in *Rudy* (1993)

"In your world, I have another name. You must learn to know me by it. That was the very reason why you were brought to Narnia, that by knowing me here for a little, you may know me better there."

–Liam Neeson as Aslan in *The Chronicles of Narnia: The Voyage of the Dawn Treader* (2010)

"God never closes one door without opening another."

–Meryl Streep as Julia Child in *Julie and Julia* (2009)

"When the Lord closes a door, somewhere He opens a window."

–Julie Andrews as Maria in *The Sound of Music* (1965)

"I keep trying to remind myself that when Jesus closes a door he opens a window."

–Mary-Louise Parker as Lillian in *Saved!* (2004)

The Greatness of God

If we put our trust in God, He will fight our battles for us. We can cast our trials on Him, and draw on His strength to get through every hardship, every sorrow, every addiction, every heartbreak. In ancient scripture we read that "he shall fight for you,"[15] and in latter-day scripture He promises "I will fight your battles."[16] On the silver screen we can find this same declaration of faith. The God we worship is ultimate and supreme, merciful and mighty. Beside His majestic glory, men are mere specs. "This is a paradox of man: compared to God, man is nothing; yet we are everything to God," President Uchtdorf explained. "While against the backdrop of infinite creation we may appear to be nothing, we have a spark of eternal fire burning within our breast."[17]

Because of this, we need not fear our Father in Heaven, but to love, trust, and obey Him. He deserves our reverence and respect and will not be mocked. "I hope you will think and feel and dress and act in ways that show reverence and respect for sacred things, sacred places, sacred occasions," encouraged Elder Christofferson.[18] We are encouraged in Matthew to not "cast ye your pearls before swine;"[19] and even Master Shifu in *Kung Fu Panda* warned us of sacrilege.

---

[15] Deuteronomy 1:30

[16] D&C 105:14

[17] Dieter F. Uchtdorf, "You Matter to Him," October 2011 General Conference.

[18] D. Todd Christofferson, "A Sense of the Sacred," *BYU Speeches,* 7 November 2004.

[19] Matthew 7:6

"The Lord of Hosts will do battle for us. Behold His mighty hand!"

–Charlton Heston as Moses in *The Ten Commandments* (1965)

"Let your armies be the rocks and the trees and the birds in the sky."

–Sean Connery as Dr. Henry Jones in *Indiana Jones and the Last Crusade* (1989)

"His god - IS God."

–Yul Brynner as Ramses in *The Ten Commandments* (1965)

"Staring up at the sky, look. It's so beautiful. So vast and endless. They're so small. My crowd, they think they're giants. They are not even dust in God's eyes."

–Kate Winslett as Rose Dewitt Bukater in *Titanic* (1997)

"No man fears to kneel before the God he trusts."

–Oliver Barker as Arthur in *King Arthur* (2017)

"I do believe that God is love, more than a stern and vengeful patriarch. He is the father who teaches us to pray, 'Forgive us our trespasses, as we forgive those who trespass against us.'"

–Jim Carrey as Bruce Nolan in *Bruce Almighty* (2003)

"God? Are you there, God? It's me... Margaret Simon. Um... I just wanted... Well...First, I've, I've heard a lot of great things about you."

-Abby Ryder Fortson as Margaret Simon in *Are You There God? It's Me, Margaret* (2023)

"We do not wash our pits in the pool of sacred tears."

–Dustin Hoffman as Master Shifu in *Kung Fu Panda* (2008)

"There is an entire generation searching for God."

–Jonathan Roumie as Lonnie Frisbee in *Jesus Revolution* (2023)

5

PRAYER, INSPIRATION, & DIVINE NATURE

In the previous chapter, we looked at what cinema says about the Father and the Son. Now, we take a look at our connection to Heaven–from the divinity within us, to our Godlike potential, to the ways we receive inspiration from the Divine and communicate back through the power of prayer.

The Divine Within

"We lived in Heaven a long time ago, it is true," sings the Primary children. Before we each were born, we frolicked among the clouds of preexistence with our Heavenly Family. It was a place of love, light, and goodness–very similar to the beautiful rest our souls will enjoy after death. It is there that we got our start. "We are made of the stuff of eternity," taught President Uchtdorf. "We are eternal beings, children of the Almighty God."[1] Jesus taught of our divine parentage and that a spark of Godliness is found inside all of us. Our humanity is intrinsically tied to our Godly origins. "Heavenly Father generously shares a portion of His divinity within us," taught Sister Rosemary M. Wixom, Primary General President. "That divine nature comes as a gift from Him with a love that only a parent can feel."[2]

We forget that we are the children of Elohim even though both prophets and movies remind us of this! "Remember who you are. You are a son or daughter of our Heavenly Father," President Monson admonished. "You came from His presence

[1] Dieter F. Uchtdorf, "Grateful in Any Circumstances," April 2014 General Conference.

[2] Rosemary M. Wixom, "Discovering the Divinity Within," October 2015 General Conference.

to live on this earth for a season, and to live in such a way that you are an example of the believers and a true light to the world."[3]

"It's easy to get turned around. This isn't the Great Beyond. It's the Great Before."

–Alice Braga as Jerry in *Soul* (2000)

"Luminous beings are we, not this crude matter."

–Frank Oz as Yoda in *Star Wars: Episode V - The Empire Strikes Back* (1980)

There's "a young carpenter's son who goes around doing magic tricks, miracles they call them. This man is different. He teaches that God is near, in every man. It's actually quite profound, some of it."

–André Morell as Sextus in *Ben-Hur* (1959)

"Why does it have to be human or divine? Maybe human is divine."

–Tom Hanks as Robert Langdon in *The DaVinci Code* (2006)

"What if we are here for a reason? What if we are part of something truly divine?"

–Chris Pine as Dr. Alex Murray in *A Wrinkle in Time* (2018)

---

[3] Thomas S. Monson, "Become a Light for All to See," *BYU Speeches,* 1 November 2011.

"In the seventeenth chapter of Luke, it is written that the kingdom of God is within man, not one man nor a group of men, but in all men! In you! You, the people, have the power, the power to create machines, the power to create happiness! You, the people, have the power to make this life free and beautiful, to make this life a wonderful adventure."

–Charlie Chaplin as A Jewish Barber in *The Great Dictator* (1940)

"He lives in you. He lives in me. He watches over everything we see."

–Robert Guillaume as Rafiki in *The Lion King* (1994)

"Great colts come from great sires."

–Margo Martindale as Miss Ham in *Secretariat* (2010)

"You have forgotten who you are and so have forgotten me. Look inside yourself, Simba. You are more than what you have become."

–James Earl Jones as Mufasa in *The Lion King* (1994)

"Don't forget where we came from."

–Pom Klementieff as Mantis in *Guardians of the Galaxy: Volume 3* (2023)

"You as ugly as an old pot, but you still a child of God…"

–Taraji P. Henson as Queenie in *The Curious Case of Benjamin Button* (2008)

"I am created by God. He designed me. So I'm not a mistake. His Son died for me, just so I could be forgiven. He picked me to be His own, so I'm chosen. He redeemed me, so I am wanted. He showed me Grace, just so I could be saved. He has a future for me, because He loves me! So I don't wonder anymore, Coach Harrison. I AM a child of God! I just wanted you to know."

–Aryn Wright-Thompson as Hannah Scott in *Overcomer* (2019)

Our Divine Potential

Not only are we children of Heavenly Parents, but because of this eternal truth the potential to become like them lies inside us all. But can flawed mortals like us really become like Father and Mother God? It is not any more unreasonable than an egg in a nest eventually progressing to become a mighty eagle. "The difference between man and God is significant—but it is one of degree, not kind," taught Elder Tad R. Callister of the Seventy. "It is the difference between an acorn and an oak tree, a rosebud and a rose, a son and a father. In truth, every man is a potential god in embryo, in fulfillment of that eternal law that like begets like."[4] Yes, remember, the mighty oak was once a nut like you!

Some movies remind us of this potential inside us all. Other films talk of our high prospective destiny. We must continue to learn and progress, so that even if it takes eons, we can

---

[4] Tad R. Callister, "Our Identity and Our Destiny," *BYU Speeches,* 14 Aug 2012.

eventually take our place among the gods. And if we are worthy, we, too, can return with honor and of our elder brother Jesus will declare, "Well done, good and faithful servant."[5]

"Our fate lives within us. You only have to be brave enough to see it."

–Kelly Macdonald as Merida in *Brave* (2012)

"Trust yourself, trust your power."

–Benedict Cumberbatch as Dr. Stephen Strange in *Doctor Strange in the Multiverse of Madness* (2022)

"Everything that made that giant tree is already contained inside this tiny little seed. All it needs is some time, a little bit of sunshine and rain, and voila! Now, you might not feel like you can do much now, but that's just because, well, you're not a tree yet. You just have to give yourself some time. You're still a seed."

–Dave Foley as Flik in *A Bug's Life* (1998)

"You are the daughter of the chief. It is time to take your place among our people. Even the wild mountain stream must someday join the big river."

–Russell Means as Powhatan in *Pocahontas* (1995)

"When you find out who you are, you find out what you need."

–Jenifer Lewis as Mama Odie in *The Princess and the Frog* (2009)

---

[5] Matthew 25:23

<u>Hercules:</u> "I've been waiting for this day a long time. . . The day I rejoin the gods."
<u>Zeus:</u> "You've done wonderfully. You really have, my boy."

–Tate Donovan as Hercules and Rip Torn as Zeus in *Hercules* (1997)

"We never know how high we are, 'till we are called to rise. And then if we are true to plan, our statures touch the skies."

–Tobey Maguire as Red Pollard in *Seabiscuit* (2003)

Inspiration Within

The internal guidance we are entitled to as spirit children of God can be a powerful presence on our path to perfection. This intuition is an invaluable compass we all can enjoy. In fact, it is absolutely essential to God's plan. Sister Neill F. Marriott of the Young Women General Presidency reminded us, "Our inspiration and intuition are necessary parts of building the kingdom of God."[6] The guidance of our hearts is ignored by our brains at our own peril, as we are reminded by both movie characters and church leaders. Having a clear head will make us all more receptive to righteousness. "We need clear minds so that the Holy Ghost can teach us what to do and what to say," stressed Elder Ballard. "We need to think straight in this world of confusion."[7]

---

[6] Neill F. Marriott, "What Shall We Do?" April 2016 General Conference.
[7] M. Russell Ballard, "Let Us Think Straight," *BYU Speeches* 20 Aug 2013.

Because of the divine spark within us, we are all guided by the Light of Christ and as members of the Church by the Holy Ghost, both of which speak to our hearts and minds and help us discern evil from good. But whenever we are taught by the Spirit, it is subtle not loud. The still, small voice within our hearts can indeed guide us. As the Lord revealed to Oliver Cowdery, "I will tell you in your mind and in your heart, by the Holy Ghost, which shall come upon you and which shall dwell in your heart."[8]

"You have more power than you realize. Don't think, and don't worry. If the time comes, you'll know what to do. It's in your blood."

–Holly Hunter as Elastigirl in *The Incredibles* (2004)

"Forget all you know, or think you know. All that you require is your intuition."

–Billy Barty as the High Aldwin in *Willow* (1988)

"You must listen to your heart and not the crowd."

–Hugh Jackman as P.T. Barnum in *The Greatest Showman* (2017)

"Just follow your heart. That's what I do."

–John Heder as Napoleon Dynamite in *Napoleon Dynamite* (2004)

---

[8] D&C 8:2

"Anyone who follows the truth in his heart never makes a mistake."

–Donald Crisp as Father John Callahan in *Knute Rockne All American* (1940)

"Sometimes what heart know, head forget."

–Pat Morita as Mr. Miyagi in *The Karate Kid II* (1986)

"Your mind is like this water my friend, when it is agitated it becomes difficult to see. But if you allow it to settle, the answer becomes clear."

–Randall Duk Kim as Master Oogway in *Kung Fu Panda* (2008)

"I know there is good in you."

–Mark Hamill as Luke Skywalker in *Star Wars: Episode VI - Return of the Jedi* (1983)

"The things you have learned will guide you, and nothing on earth can silence the quiet voice still inside you. . . that voice inside is who you are."

–Rachel House as Gramma Tala in *Moana* (2016)

Listen to the Spirit

So, whether it is the Light of Christ that we all have, the impressions of the Holy Ghost that all hearers of truth enjoy, or the gift of the Holy Ghost that confirmed members of the Church receive, we can listen and be guided by the Spirit. Like our conscience, too many today ignore these quiet spiritual impressions. These promptings are there, but only to those who will listen. Earning the right to the Spirit includes humility. "An individual who is arrogant or who lets his or her emotions influence decisions will not be powerfully led by the Spirit," said Elder Richard G. Scott of the Twelve.[9] These spiritual promptings are worth humbling ourselves for, however. Listening to this still, small voice is encouraged in many films.

"Let your heart guide you. It whispers so listen closely."
–Helen Shaver as Littlefoot's Mother in *The Land Before Time* (1988)

"A conscience is that still small voice people won't listen to. That's just the trouble with the world today."
–Cliff Edwards as Jiminy Cricket in *Pinocchio* (1940)

"Boys, you must strive to find your own voice. Because the longer you wait to begin, the less likely you are to find it at all."
–Robin Williams as John Keating in *Dead Poets Society* (1989)

"Inspiration is a gift, a gift that has to be earned."
–Robert De Niro as Rudy in *Joy* (2015)

"Great, kid. Don't get cocky."
–Harrison Ford as Han Solo in *Star Wars: Episode IV - A New Hope* (1977)

---

9 Richard G. Scott, "How to Obtain Revelation and Inspiration for Your Personal Life," April 2012 General Conference.

"God whispers into the ears of some men, but he shouts into mine."

–Ed Harris as Ludwig van Beethoven in *Copying Beethoven* (2006)

"There is a higher voice that speaks through him, and he will always answer its call."

–Olive Deering as Miriam in *Samson and Delilah* (1949)

"The night is filled with Thy voice. Here am I. What wouldst Thou demand of me?"

–George C. Scott as Abraham in *The Bible: In the Beginning...* (1966)

"All around you are spirits, child. They live in the earth, the water, the sky. If you listen, they will guide you. Listen with your heart, you will understand."

–Linda Hunt as Grandmother Willow in *Pocahontas* (1995)

"Feel the force feeling through you, Rey."

–Samuel L. Jackson as Mace Windu in *Star Wars: Episode IX - The Rise of Skywalker* (2019)

"I'm one with the Force. The Force is with me."

–Donnie Yen as Chirrut Îmwe in *Rogue One: A Star Wars Story* (2016)

Praying for Help

If inspiration and the voice of the Spirit is one way God reaches out to us, how do we reach up to Him? Through prayer, of course! "We can reach into the heavens and personally commune with the Infinite," declared Elder Wirthlin.[10] Life can be tough, but our Father in Heaven has given us an open invitation to "reach for the sky." He is always there, eager to hear from His children. Praying for help through life's trials is one of the greatest reasons we all fall to our knees and plead to the heavens.

Like in real life, some prayers in the movies are simple and others are quite profound and offered on behalf of others. The neighbors and family of George Bailey offer up a variety of heartfelt prayers for him at the opening of *It's a Wonderful Life*, for example. Children of God humbling themselves surely causes Heaven to take note. In the movies, nuns are also great at teaching us about prayer. But prayer can often be much simpler than all of these examples. If we humble ourselves through prayer, approaching him like the Father and Friend that he is, He will show His will for us and teach.

"Reach for the sky!"
–Tim Allen as Buzz Lightyear in *Toy Story* (1995)

"Do you believe in prayer?"
–James Stewart as Buttons in *The Greatest Show on Earth* (1952)

---

[10] Joseph B. Wirthlin, "One Step after Another," October 2001 General Conference.

"Taking your appeal to a higher authority?"
–Robert Prosky as Father Cavanaugh in *Rudy* (1993)

"If you can take it, you can make it. If you can't take it, you can pray about it."
–Jack O'Connell as Prisoner of War Louis Zamperini in *Unbroken* (2014)

"Prayer always seems to be the last thing we do when it should be the first."
–Pat Boone as Walter Wesley in *God's Not Dead 2* (2016)

"Sometimes, we have to ask for help. And that's okay."
–Tom Hanks as Fred Rogers in *A Beautiful Day in the Neighborhood* (2019)

"Elohim, God on high, can you hear your people cry? Help us now, this dark hour. Deliver us, hear our call, deliver us, Lord of all!"
–Val Kilmer as Moses in *The Prince of Egypt* (1998)

"I ask for nothing, I can get by, but I know so many less lucky than I. Please help my people, the poor and down trod."
–Heidi Mollenhaur as Esmerelda's singing voice in *The Hunchback of Notre Dame* (1996)

"God on high, hear my prayer. In my need, you have always been there."

–Hugh Jackman as Jean Valjean in *Les Misérables* (2012)

"God... God... Dear Father in Heaven. I'm not a praying man, but if you're up there and you can hear me, show me the way. I'm at the end of my rope. Show me the way, God."

–James Stewart as George Bailey in *It's a Wonderful Life* (1946)

"If you answer my prayers...you get me through this...I swear...I'll do whatever you want. I'll dedicate my life to you. Please…"

–Jack O'Connell as Prisoner of War Louis Zamperini in *Unbroken* (2014)

"Is it too late to say a prayer? I'd say one for myself, but I have never prayed in my life... no one ever taught me how."

–Sandra Bullock as Astronaut Ryan Stone in *Gravity* (2013)

"We are nuns. We seek solutions through prayer. We pray. . . We pray for good things. Food for the hungry."

–Maggie Smith as Mother Superior in *Sister Act* (1992)

"If you call Jesus, His line is never busy."

–Isaac Hayes as Preacher Hurn in *Once Upon a Time . . . When We Were Colored* (1995)

"And now, dear God, about Liesl (as the oldest Von Trapp child sneaked into the house through Maria's window). Help her know that I'm her friend . . . and help her tell me what she's been up to."

–Julie Andrews as Fräulein Maria in *The Sound of Music* (1965)

"E.T. phone home."

–Pat Welsh as E.T. in *E.T. the Extra-Terrestrial* (1982)

"They want you to say the grace! The blessing!"

–William Hickey as Uncle Lewis to Aunt Bethany in *National Lampoon's Christmas Vacation* (1989)

"Prayer is a powerful thing. And it turns out God has much bigger plans for you."

–Michael Tait as The Newsboy in *God's Not Dead 2* (2016)

"Heavenly Father. We thank you for all your many blessings on this family. . ."

–Sandra Bullock as Leigh Anne Tuohy in *The Blind Side* (2009)

"Prayer doesn't have to be a list of requests. It can just be the sound of somebody's voice, hoping somebody's listening."

–Keegan-Michael Key as Zach the Donkey in *The Star* (2017)

"Always keep a prayer in your pocket."

–Meryl Streep as Aunt March in *Little Women* (2019)

"Father, thank you for the gathering of friends. Father, we give thanks for all the choices we've made, because that's what makes us who we are. Let us forever cherish the loved ones we've lost along the way. Thank you for the little angel, the newest addition to our family. Thank you for bringing Letty home. And most of all, thank you for fast cars."

–Tyrese Gibson as Roman Pearce in *Fast & Furious 6* (2013)

"You prayed for a tailwind. Perhaps there are others at sea praying for a headwind. We should make it possible for God to bless both by praying only for a good wind!"

–Joe Folau as Feki in *The Other Side of Heaven* (2001)

"Are you there, God? It's me, Margaret . . . . Let me just be normal and regular like everybody else. Just please, please, please, please, please, please, please! Amen."

-Abby Ryder Fortson as Margaret Simon in *Are You There God? It's Me, Margaret* (2023)

"Bless the seven little men who have been so kind to me. And, and may my dreams come true. Amen. Oh yes, and please make Grumpy like me."

–Adriana Caselotti as Snow White in *Snow White and the Seven Dwarfs* (1937)

How Prayers are Answered

Elder John H. Groberg of the Seventy spoke in both real life and through the movie based on his life about the power of our interrelation with God. Prayer, and listening for God's answer, is the heart of that connection. The gospel and films, however, both teach that God answers in His own way. Elder Brook P. Hales of the Seventy taught "as an all-knowing, loving Father, He answers our prayers perfectly, according to His infinite wisdom, and in ways that will be to our ultimate benefit and blessing."[11] The movies also remind us that God will answer prayers according to His timing. While sometimes that timing requires us to exercise patience, other times the answer may come quickly.

When those answers to prayer do come, the connections to Heaven are indeed wonderful. "God is eagerly waiting for the chance to answer your prayers and fulfill your dreams, just as He always has," taught Elder Holland. "But He can't if you don't pray, and He can't if you don't dream."[12] So, don't forget to pray and to involve our Heavenly Father in your hopes and dreams.

"Only when our lips are silent, can our prayers truly be heard."
–Maggie Smith as Mother Superior in *Sister Act* (1992)

---

[11] Brook P. Hales, "Answers to Prayer," April 2019 General Conference.
[12] Jeffrey R. Holland, "This, the Greatest of All Dispensations," Church Educational System fireside, 12 Sep 2004.

"There is a connection between heaven and earth. Finding that connection gives meaning to everything, including death. Losing that connection makes everything lose meaning, including life."

–Christopher Gorham as John Groberg in *The Other Side of Heaven* (2001)[13]

"I've been discussing the whole thing with God. We're very close now, He and I."

–Heather Beers as Charlene 'Charly' Riley in *Charly* (2002)

"More than three thousand years ago a man named Job complained to God about all his troubles and the Bible tells us that God answered."

–Diane Lane as Penny Chenery in *Secretariat* (2010)

"Let me ask you something. If someone prays for patience, you think God gives them patience? Or does he give them the opportunity to be patient? If he prayed for courage, does God give him courage, or does he give him opportunities to be courageous? If someone prayed for the family to be closer, do you think God zaps them with warm fuzzy feelings, or does he give them opportunities to love each other?"

–Morgan Freeman as God in *Evan Almighty* (2007)

---

[13] See also John H. Groberg, "The Other Side of Heaven," *BYU Speeches*, 4 Dec 2001.

Grace: "Recently when I've been praying, it's like Jesus isn't letting me feel His presence. Usually I can almost reach out and touch Him but... but right now it's like... it's like He's a million miles away."
Walter: "Honey, you of all people should realize when you're going through something really hard, the teacher is always quiet during the test."

–Melissa Joan Hart as Grace Wesley, Pat Boone as Walter Wesley in *God's Not Dead 2* (2016)

"Praying is something we do in our time. The answers come in God's time."

–Robert Prosky as Father Cavanaugh in *Rudy* (1993)

"I asked him to pray for me. I figure anyone who is going through what he is going through must be awfully close to God."

–Tom Hanks as Mr. Rogers in *A Beautiful Day in the Neighborhood* (2019)

"And please let someone find my bottle. There's a message in it. Because running away isn't working. Amen." No sooner does she finish her prayer and wipe away her tears then the two mice, Bernard and Bianca, introduce themselves as her rescuers.

–Michelle Stacy as Penny in *The Rescuers* (1977)

"I do believe in God. And I know that He hears your prayers, even if sometimes the answer is 'no'."

–David Kelly as Grandpa Joe in *Charlie and the Chocolate Factory* (2005)

"It's as though all the cosmic tumblers have clicked into place and the universe opens itself up for a few seconds to show you what's possible."

–Kevin Costner as Ray Kinsella in *Field of Dreams* (1989)

"That's not why I pray, Harry. I pray because I can't help myself. I pray because I'm helpless. I pray because the need flows out of me all the time, waking and sleeping. It doesn't change God, it changes me."

–Anthony Hopkins as Jack (C.S. Lewis) in *Shadowlands* (1993

6

HOPE, CHANGE, & MIRACLES

The Book of Mormon prophet Moroni, living in a dark time, must have written about hope frequently because that was a light he was personally clinging to. God-fearing saints must "with surety hope for a better world," he said in Ether.[1] We "must press forward," said another prophet, Nephi, "having a perfect brightness of hope."[2] The movies are chock-full of characters encouraging us to not only have hope, but to embrace change, and to believe in miracles. In fact, like the gospel, the silver screen often encourages us to be that miracle in the lives of others.

Need for Hope

As spiritual beings having a mortal experience, we must have hope in life. "There is always hope," said Elder Groberg. "No matter how dismal things appear, no matter how problem-prone we seem to be, no matter what reversals and setbacks we suffer, there is always hope. Hope is the thing that keeps us going," he said.[3] There is an innate need within our souls to be hopeful–we must believe that things can get better, that the days will get brighter, that the good guys will win in the end.

Yet, when the light of hope goes out, we are spiritually weaker. "Hope has the power to fill our lives with happiness," said President Uchtdorf. "Its absence—when this desire of our heart is delayed—can make 'the heart sick.'"[4] The movies also show

---

[1] Ether 12:4
[2] 2 Nephi 31:20
[3] John H. Groberg, "There is Always Hope," *BYU Speeches,* 3 June 1984.
[4] Dieter F. Uchtdorf, "The Infinite Power of Hope," October 2008 General Conference.

us the tragedy of hopelessness. Moroni wrote of this dangerous state when he said, "And if ye have no hope ye must needs be in despair."[5] Cinema agrees and tells us that we all need hope.

"You don't lose hope, love. If you do, you lose everything."

–Angela Lansbury as Mrs. Potts in *Beauty and the Beast* (1991)

"That's the thing about atheism. It doesn't take away the pain... just takes away the hope."

–Pat Boone as Walter Wesley in *God's Not Dead 2* (2016)

"Hope is like the sun. If you only believe it when you see it you'll never make it through the night."

–Carrie Fisher as Princess Leia Organa in *Star Wars: Episode VIII - The Last Jedi* (2017)

"You never know. You hope for the best and make do with what you get."

–Samuel L. Jackson as Nick Fury in *Avengers: Age of Ultron* (2015)

Frodo: "What are we holding onto, Sam?"
Sam: "That there's some good in this world, Mr. Frodo, and it's worth fighting for."

–Elijah Wood as Frodo Baggins and Sean Astin as Samwise Gamgee in *The Lord of the Rings: The Two Towers* (2002)

---

[5] Moroni 10:22

"People have begun to lose their hopes and forget their dreams. . . It's the emptiness that's left. It's like a despair, destroying this world."

–Alan Oppenheimer as G'Mork in *The NeverEnding Story* (1984)

"Having dreams is what makes life tolerable."

–Christopher Reed as Pete in *Rudy* (1993)

"We need you to hope again."

–Patrick Stewart as Professor X in *X-Men Days of Future Past* (2014)

"We will find hope in the impossible."

–Zachary Quinto as Spock in *Star Trek Beyond* (2016)

"May the Force be with you."

–Alex McCrindle as General Dodonna in *Star Wars: Episode IV - A New Hope* (1977)

Power of Hope

The act of wishing a movie hero "good luck" as they set out on a new adventure, or invoking "May the Force be with you," as the case may be, is encouraging positive vibes and the power of hope. The hope that things will get better, that situations will work out for the best is always impactful. Sister Reyna I. Aburto of the Relief Society General Presidency testified that "the sun will shine again, and things will not be difficult forever."[6] The gospel teaches that while there needs to be opposition in all things, the opposition doesn't need to last forever. "Hope sustains us through despair," taught President Uchtdorf. "Hope teaches that there is reason to rejoice even when all seems dark around us."[7] President Hinckley lived with this hopeful optimism in his heart. "Oh, things will work out," he would often say to his associates with a smile, even amidst pressing problems. "Oh, it will work out. And the best is yet to come."[8]

"Hope, it is the only thing stronger than fear."
–Donald Sutherland as President Snow in *The Hunger Games* (2012)

"There should be no boundaries to human endeavor. We are all different. However bad life may seem, there is always something you can do, and succeed at. While there's life, there is hope."
–Eddie Redmayne as Stephen Hawking in *The Theory of Everything* (2014)

"Hope is not a strategy."
–Henry Cavill as August Walker in *Mission Impossible: Fallout* (2018)

---

[6] Reyna I. Aburto, "Heartbreak and Hope" video released on lds.org 19 July 2018.
[7] Dieter F. Uchtdorf, "The Infinite Power of Hope," October 2008 General Conference.
[8] Quoted in Henry B. Eyring, "Things Will Work Out," *In Memoriam: President Gordon B. Hinckley,* March 2008.

"The symbol of the house of El means hope. Embodied within that hope is the fundamental belief in the potential for every person to be a force for good."

–Russell Crowe as Jor-El in *Man of Steel* (2013)

"Even the darkest night will end and the sun will rise."

–Eddie Redmayne as Marius Pontmercy in *Les Misérables* (2012)

"I assure you, brother. The sun will shine on us again."

–Tom Hiddleston as Loki in *Avengers: Infinity War* (2018)

"The night is darkest just before the dawn. And I promise you, the dawn is coming."

–Aaron Eckhart as Harvey Dent in *The Dark Knight* (2008)

"Hope is not lost today . . . it is found."

–Carrie Fisher as Princess Leia Organa in *Star Wars: Episode VII - The Force Awakens* (2015)

Inevitability of Change

Both the gospel and the movies teach us that nothing is as inevitable as change. The world changed over the eons of creation and still changes. The gospel has to change as revelation continues to distill from heaven and the kingdom of God rolls forth. We have to change as individuals if we are to ever reach our divine potential. "Our world is constantly changing . . . ever since its creation—geologically and geographically," taught President Nelson. "And its populations are changing—politically and spiritually."[9]

Many of us struggle with change and like things to stay as they are. We get comfortable with what we know, and the uncertainty of a shifting world can be troubling. "There is a tendency to think of change as the enemy," said Elder Ashton. "Many of us are suspect of change and will often fight and resist it before we have even discovered what the actual effects will be. When change is thought through carefully, it can produce the most rewarding and profound experiences in life."[10] He's not wrong, and movie personas from Shmi Skywalker to Olaf the Snowman teach us this, as well. "Throughout our lives, we must deal with change," President Monson insisted.[11]

"Things change. Always do."

–Vernon Washington as Otis in *The Last Starfighter* (1984)

"Honey, it's life. Life IS change."

–America Ferrera as Gloria in *Barbie* (2023)

[9] Russel M. Nelson, "Constancy amid Change," October 1993 General Conference.

[10] Marvin J. Ashton, "Progress through Change," October 1979 General Conference.

[11] Thomas S. Monson, "Finding Joy in the Journey," October 2008 General Conference.

"What I love most about rivers is you can't step in the same river twice. The water's always changing, always flowing."

–Irene Bedard as Pocahontas in *Pocahontas* (1995)

"You can't stop change any more than you can stop the suns from setting."

–Pernilla August as Shmi Skywalker in *Star Wars: Episode I - The Phantom Menace* (1999)

"How I wish it could stay this way forever, and yet change mocks us with her beauty."

–Josh Gad as Olaf in *Frozen 2* (2019)

"After all . . . tomorrow is another day."

–Vivien Leigh as Scarlett O'Hara in *Gone with the Wind* (1939)

You Can Change

The gospel is all about change. We can all be "born again" and accept our place among the disciples of Jesus Christ. We can exercise our agency to become who we want to become. "You can change! You can be anything you want to be in righteousness," said Elder Holland. "You can change anything you want to change, and you can do it very fast," he said.[12]

It is an empowering thought to know that we can decide and act to be better than we were yesterday. "Do you want to change the

[12]Jeffrey R. Holland, "For Times of Trouble," *BYU Speeches*, 18 Mar 1980.

shape of your life?" asked Elder Uchtdorf. "Change the shape of your day. Do you want to change your day? Change this hour. Change what you think, feel, and do at this very moment."[13] From Captain Kirk to Rocky Balboa, the movies, too, tell us that we have the power to change.

"We change. We have to. Or we spend the rest of our lives fighting the same battles."

–Chris Pine as Captain James T. Kirk in *Star Trek Beyond* (2016)

"If I can change, and you can change, everybody can change."

–Sylvester Stallone as Rocky Balboa in *Rocky IV* (1985)

"The Na'vi say that every person is born twice. The second time is when you earn your place among the people...forever."

–Sam Worthington as Jake Sully in *Avatar* (2009)

"Somebody's life's about to change"

–Leonardo DiCaprio as Jack Dawson in *Titanic* (1997)

"Growing up means adapting. Puzzling out your world and your place."

–Josh Gad as Olaf in *Frozen 2* (2019)

---

[13] Dieter F. Uchtdorf, "Daily Restoration," October 2021 General Conference.

"Change is nature, Dad. The part that we can influence. And it starts when we decide."

–Ryan Reynolds as Guy in *The Croods* (2013)

"Those who never change their mind never change anything."

–Gary Oldman as Winston Churchill in *Darkest Hour* (2017)

"We expand or die!"

–Steve Coogan as Octavius in *Night at the Museum* (2006)

Miracles are Everywhere

From the parting of the Red Sea to Balaam's talking donkey in the book of Numbers, the scriptures are filled with miracles. "Have miracles ceased?" asked Moroni around 400 A.D. "Behold I say unto you, Nay."[14] This is true not just in ancient times, but today, as well. We still live in a world filled with miracles, for those who spiritually pay attention. "There will always be plenty of miracles if we have eyes to see and ears to hear," said President Howard W. Hunter. "As a result of the many miracles in our lives, we should be more humble and more grateful, more kind and more believing," he said.[15]

Movies talk about miracles, and so do modern apostles. "Many of you have witnessed miracles," declared Elder Ronald A.

---

[14] Moroni 7:29

[15] Howard W. Hunter, "The God That Doest Wonders," April 1989 General Conference.

Rasband of the Twelve, "more than you realize."[16] Often we just call these coincidences, but both Master Oogway and Apostle David A. Bednar would disagree. "The tender mercies of the Lord are real and they do not occur randomly or merely by coincidence," Elder Bednar said.[17]

"Well, I've got a talking donkey."

–Kathleen Freeman as Old Woman in *Shrek* (2001)

"There are no coincidences in this world."

–Randall Duk Kim as Master Oogway in *Kung Fu Panda* (2008)

"Some people don't think miracles happen; well, they do."

–Tom Hanks as Forrest Gump in *Forrest Gump* (1994)

"Miracles happen all the time!"

–Lily James as Ellie Appleton in *Yesterday* (2019)

"I don't know, but it has happened -- at a time when we really don't see many miraculous things. Maybe we do. Maybe they're all right there around us every day, we just don't know where to look."

–Gary Basaraba as Homer Zuckerman in *Charlotte's Web* (2006)

---

16 Ronald A. Rasband, "Behold! I Am a God of Miracles," April 2021 General Conference.

17 David A. Bednar, "The Tender Mercies of the Lord," April 2005 General Conference.

"Is anything too hard for the Lord?"

–Peter O'Toole as one of The Three Angels in *The Bible: In the Beginning...* (1966)

"Parting a soup is not a miracle, Bruce. It's a magic trick. Now, a single mom who works two full-time jobs, and still finds the time to pick up her kid at soccer practice, that's a miracle. A teenager that says 'no' to drugs and 'yes' to an education, that's a miracle."

–Morgan Freeman as God in *Bruce Almighty* (2003)

"Albert Einstein said there are only two ways to live your life. One is as though nothing is a miracle and the other is as though everything is a miracle. I'm the first to tell you I wasn't living my life as though everything is a miracle. I missed a lot. Miracles are everywhere."

–Jennifer Garner as Christy Beam in *Miracles from Heaven* (2016)

Be the Miracle

Miracles on earth often occur because of the godly stepping up to serve as God would. "As we search, pray, and believe, we will recognize miracles in our lives and become miracle workers in the lives of others," said Young Women's General President Susan Winder Tanner.[18] Prophets and protagonists alike implore us to be a miracle in the lives of our fellow sisters and brothers.

[18] Susan W. Tanner, "All Things Shall Work Together for Your Good," April 2004 General Conference.

"The Lord answers our prayers, but it is usually through another person that he meets our needs," President Spencer W. Kimball famously said.[19]

"People want me to do everything for them. What they don't realize is that they have the power. You want to see a miracle? Be the miracle."

–Morgan Freeman as God in *Bruce Almighty* (2003)

"Sometimes God uses the unlikely to perform miracles."

–Sandra Bullock as Leigh Anne Tuohy in *The Blind Side* (2009)

"That old star can only take you part of the way. You got to help him with some hard work of your own."

–Terrence Howard as James in *The Princess and the Frog* (2009)

"Sometimes miracles are just good people with kind hearts."

–Kevin Spacey as Eugene Simonet in *Pay It Forward* (2000)

"You rush a miracle man, you get rotten miracles."

--Billy Crystal as Miracle Max in *The Princess Bride* (1987)

---

[19] Quoted in Richard P. Lindsay, "Ye Have Done It unto Me," April 1990 General Conference.

Landon: "I'm sorry she never got her miracle."
Reverend Sullivan: "She did. It was you."

–Shane West as Landon and Peter Coyote as Reverend Sullivan in *A Walk to Remember* (2002)

"Miracles are made by people who refuse to stop believing."

–Kristen Wiig as Cheryl Melhoff in *The Secret Life of Walter Mitty* (2013)

7

CHOICE & ACCOUNTABILITY

Both movies and the gospel teach us of the gift of agency, that our choices have consequences, to choose the right even though some choices are difficult, and that ultimately we decide our own destiny. After all, we are merely the sum of our choices. "I can't stress too strongly that decisions determine destiny," taught President Monson. "You can't make eternal decisions without eternal consequences."[1] And that is prophetic counsel that Albus Dumbledore, Obi-Wan Kenobi, and even Thor could agree with.

Gift of Agency

When our Heavenly Parents planned this world for us to experience mortality away from their immediate presence, they did so in large part to let us exercise our agency. "Next to life itself, free agency is God's greatest gift to mankind," taught Elder L. Tom Perry of the Twelve.[2] We are free to choose in this life light or darkness, goodness or evil. "God desires, expects, and directs that each of His children choose for himself or herself," said another apostle, Elder Dale G. Renlund. "He will not force us," he said.[3]

We are the masters of our own fate. We are originals who determine our own paths. We are "free according to the flesh," we read in the Book of Mormon, "free to choose liberty and

---

[1] Thomas S. Monson, "Decisions Determine Destiny," *BYU Speeches*, 6 November 2005.

[2] L. Tom Perry, "Obedience to Law is Liberty," April 2013 General Conference.

[3] Dale G. Renlund, "Choose You This Day," October 2018 General Conference.

eternal life . . . or captivity and death."[4] These are themes seen repeatedly on the big screen. Such freedom and agency are indeed gifts! As President Nelson put it, "You get to decide what kind of life you want to live forever."[5]

"To be free. To be my own master. Such a thing would be greater than all the magic and all the treasures in all the world."
–Robin Williams as the Genie in *Aladdin* (1992)

"I am the master of my fate - I am the captain of my soul."
–Morgan Freeman as Nelson Mandela quoting William Ernest Henley in *Invictus* (2009)

"You cannot let your father's actions define your life. You get to decide what kind of King you want to be."
–Lupita Nyong'o as Nakia in *Black Panther* (2018)

"I am the one thing in life I can control. I am inimitable, I am an original."
–Leslie Odom Jr. as Aaron Burr in *Hamilton* (2020)

"You must choose your own path."
–Russell Means as Chief Powhatan in *Pocahontas* (1995)

---

[4] 2 Nephi 2:27

[5] Quoted in Mary Richards, "President Nelson asks young adults, 'Decide what kind of life you want to live forever'," *Church News*, online at churchofjesuschrist.org accessed 10 June 2023.

"I need to figure out exactly who I am. I want to choose my own path."

–Chris Hemsworth as Thor in *Thor: Love and Thunder* (2022)

"You must learn to choose between right and wrong."

–Evelyn Venable as the Blue Fairy in *Pinocchio* (1940)

"Remember, with great power comes great responsibility."

–Cliff Robertson as Uncle Ben in *Spider-Man* (2002)

"When an individual acquires great power, the use or misuse of that power is everything."

–Patrick Stewart as Professor X in *X-Men: The Last Stand* (2006)

"Life is choice. You can choose to be a victim or anything else you'd like to be."

–Nick Nolte as Socrates in *Peaceful Warrior* (2006)

Our Choices Have Consequences

"Discipleship is not about doing things perfectly; it's about doing things intentionally," said Elder Uchtdorf. "It is your choices that show what you truly are, far more than your abilities," he said, paraphrasing Albus Dumbledore.[6] Many movies teach us that our choices do indeed have consequences.

In the hymn we sing, "Do what is right, let the consequence follow." And indeed, the consequences do! Good things come of responsible choices; problems grow as we choose poorly. President Hinckley taught, "Don't make the kinds of mistakes that will bring regret. You can be wise and happy or stupid and miserable. The choice is yours."[7] When it comes to choices, we will reap what we sow.

"It is not our abilities that show what we truly are … it is our choices."

–Richard Harris as Albus Dumbledore in *Harry Potter and the Chamber of Secrets* (2002)

"Our lives are the sum of our choices."

–Henry Czerny as Eugene Kittridge in *Mission: Impossible - Dead Reckoning Part One* (2023)

"Our choices make us who we are, don't they?"

–Will Ferrell as Present in *Spirited* (2022)

"He Chose...Poorly."

–Robert Eddison as Grail Knight in *Indiana Jones and the Last Crusade* (1989)

---

[6] Dieter F. Uchtdorf, "Your Great Adventure," October 2019 General Conference.

[7] Quoted by Stephanie Long in "Prophet, Church Leaders Counsel Youth at Fireside," *Ensign*, March 2007.

"Stupid is as stupid does."

–Tom Hanks as Forrest Gump in *Forrest Gump* (1994)

"The choices we make dictate the life we lead, 'to thine own self be true'."

–Danny DeVito as Bill Rago in *Renaissance Man* (1994)

"Sometimes your whole life boils down to one insane move."

–Sam Worthington as Jake Sully in *Avatar* (2009)

"Who's the more foolish: the fool, or the fool who follows him?"

–Alec Guinness as Obi-Wan Kenobi in *Star Wars: Episode IV - A New Hope* (1977)

Alice: "I was just wondering if you could help me find my way."
Cheshire Cat: "Well that depends on where you want to get to."
Alice: "Oh, it really doesn't matter, as long as…"
Cheshire Cat: "Then it really doesn't matter which way you go."

–Kathryn Beaumont and Sterling Holloway as Alice and Cheshire Cat in *Alice in Wonderland* (1951)

Choose the Right

The scriptures and countless church leaders encourage us to choose the right. Even in song, we sing "Choose the right, when a choice is placed before you." Despite having our agency in life, it is all a big test to see if we will choose the good path when we come to life's crossroads. Many films also encourage us to do the right thing, follow paths of light, and decide wisely.

"Occasionally we are given true-and-false tests in life—clear right and wrong choices—moments of truth," said Sister Michelle D. Craig of the Young Women General Presidency. "At those moments, stand up. Stand tall. Choose with courage."[8] Not only should we choose the right, but we should jump to it promptly! "Let us do the right thing at the right time, without delay," admonished Elder José L. Alonso of the Seventy.[9]

"It's not who you are underneath, it's what you do that defines you."

–Katie Holmes as Rachel Dawes in *Batman Begins* (2005)

"There will come a time when you have a chance to do the right thing."

–Keira Knightly as Elizabeth Swann in *Pirates of the Caribbean: Dead Man's Chest* (2006)

"Just do the next right thing."

–Kristen Bell as Anna in *Frozen 2* (2019)

---

[8] Quoted by Marianne Holman Prescott, "Sister Craig Shares 3 Ways to Prioritize "Never-Ending To-Do Lists," *Church News,* 13 December 2018.

[9] José L. Alonso, "Doing the Right Thing at the Right Time, without Delay," October 2011 General Conference.

"Just follow the Yellow Brick Road."

–Billy Burke as Glinda in *The Wizard of Oz* (1939)

"It is the quality of one's convictions that determines success, not the number of followers."

–David Thewlis as Remus Lupin in *Harry Potter and the Half-Blood Prince* (2009)

"You must choose, but choose wisely."

–Sean Connery as Dr. Henry Jones in *Indiana Jones and the Last Crusade* (1989)

"My daddy once said 'If you don't make a choice, the choice makes you.'"

–Nicholas Cage as Johnny Blaze in *Ghost Rider* (2007)

"Sometimes the best course of action is to do nothing, but sometimes, doing nothing is the worst course of action."

–Christian Bale as Bruce Wayne in *The Dark Knight* (2008)

"You do somethin' for the right reasons, nothing can stop you."

–Thomas Haden Church as Duncan Mee in *We Bought a Zoo* (2011)

"You can't cherry pick the Bible, choosing which parts you want to believe."

–Andrew Rannells as Trent Oliver in *The Prom* (2020)

"When God tells you what to do, you cannot hesitate."

–Bill Camp as Vampiro in *Sound of Freedom* (2023)

"It's the choices that make us who we are, and we can always choose to do what's right."

–Tobey Maguire as Peter Parker in *Spider-Man 3* (2007)

Difficult Choices

Not only are we asked to choose the right, but sometimes choosing the right is the tougher decision. "The ideal course of life is not always easy," said Elder Wirthlin. "Comparatively few will find it and complete it," he said.[10] But this is the path of goodness encouraged by parents, church leaders, and movie heroes alike.

So, once we know the right path to select, how do we summon the courage to choose the better part? "When it comes right down to it, it is a matter of strong resolve," taught Elder Joe J. Christensen of the Seventy.[11] Even screen villains like Thanos and Henri Ducard would agree with that. So let us make the hard choices. Let us choose the light. "May we ever choose the harder right instead of the easier wrong." plead President Monson.[12]

---

[10] Joseph B. Wirthlin, "Running your Marathon," October 1989 General Conference.

[11] Joe J. Christensen, "I Resolve," *The New Era,* January 1998.

[12] Thomas S. Monson, "Choices," April 2016 General Conference.

"Life's full of tough choices, isn't it?"

–Melissa McCarthy as Ursula the Sea Witch in *The Little Mermaid* (2023)

"Sometimes the right path is not the easiest one."

–Linda Hunt as Grandmother Willow in *Pocahontas* (1995)

"How can he find his own way if he does not learn to choose a path?"

–Adil Hussain as Santosh Patel in *Life of Pi* (2012)

"Whatever comes our way, whatever battle we have raging inside us, we always have a choice."

–Tobey Maguire as Peter Parker in *Spider-Man 3* (2007)

"Now you see the world is full of temptations. . . Take the straight and narrow path and if you start to slide give a little whistle! Give a little whistle! And always let your conscience be your guide."

–Cliff Edwards as Jiminy Cricket in *Pinocchio* (1940)

"Dark times lie ahead of us and there will be a time when we must choose between what is easy and what is right."

–Michael Gambon as Albus Dumbledore in *Harry Potter and the Goblet of Fire* (2005)

"The hardest choices require the strongest wills."

–Josh Brolin as Thanos in *Avengers: Infinity War* (2018)

"The training is nothing! The will is everything!"

–Liam Neeson as Henri Ducard in *Batman Begins* (2005)

"Even a good decision, if made for the wrong reasons, can be a wrong decision."

–Jonathan Pryce as Governor Swann in *Pirates of the Caribbean: The Curse of the Black Pearl* (2003)

"Every day you're not dead in the ground, when you wake up in the morning, you're gonna have to make some decisions."

–Cicely Tyson as Constantine Jefferson in *The Help* (2011)

"Now which way do we go?"

–Judy Garland as Dorothy Gale in *The Wizard of Oz* (1939)

8

FAMILY, FRIENDS, & NEIGHBORS

The Primary children summarize the powerful doctrine in song, "God gave us families to help us become what He wants us to be."[1] Jesus Christ told us "Ye are my friends."[2] He taught us to "love thy neighbor as thyself."[3] Looking beyond ourselves and strengthening our relationships with family, friends, and neighbors is at the heart of both the gospel and many movies.

Families are Difficult but Worth It

Family life is wonderful, but at times tough. Egos, emotions, and living in close quarters all bring their challenges. Nephi knew all about this; so did Joseph the son of Jacob. "In spite of how difficult family life can be at times, the work we do in our families is of the utmost importance," taught Sister Virginia U. Jensen of the Relief Society General Presidency. "Don't allow the difficulties inherent in family life to unduly discourage you or to impact the love which we can share in families," she said.[4] Even superheroes admit that families at times can be arduous. Yet, prophets point out that they are worth the effort. "The greatest of the Lord's work you brethren will ever do will be within the walls of your own home," declared President Lee to a priesthood meeting. "Don't neglect your wives, you brethren. Don't neglect your children."[5]

---

1 Matthew Neeley, "The Family Is of God," *Friend*, October 2008.
2 John 15:14
3 Matthew 22:39
4 Virginia U. Jensen, "Stand Firm," October 2001 General Conference.
5 Harold B. Lee, "Follow the Leadership of the Church," April 1973 General Conference.

"Families can be tough."

–Chris Hemsworth as Thor in *Avengers: Infinity War* (2018)

"I've been a lousy father, blind to what I have. So obsessed with being undervalued that I undervalued all of you."

–Craig T. Nelson as Mr. Incredible in *The Incredibles* (2004)

"How you feel about your family is a complicated thing–especially with an older brother."

–Macauley Culkin as Kevin McCallister in *Home Alone* (1990)

"Hmm. So, that's how it is in their family."

–Jeffrey Duncan Jones as Ed Rooney in *Ferris Bueller's Day Off* (1986)

"In this house, we believe in second chances, we believe in redemption, and we believe in family."

–Albert Brooks as Marlin in *Finding Dory* (2016)

"Being perfect is not about that scoreboard out there. It's not about winning. It's about you and your relationship with yourself, your family and your friends."

–Billy Bob Thornton as Coach Gary Gaines in *Friday Night Lights* (2004)

The Power of Family and Home

The Church of Jesus Christ is known for its emphasis on families–because God has revealed through His prophets that there is immense power in family and home. "Our family is the focus of our greatest work and joy in this life; so will it be throughout all eternity," said President Nelson.[6] "Happiness is found at home," pointed out President Monson, "The home is the laboratory of our lives, and what we learn there largely determines what we do when we leave there."[7] And of course, President David O. McKay famously said "No other success can compensate for failure in the home. The poorest shack in which love prevails over a united family is of greater value to God and future humanity than any other riches. In such a home God can work miracles and will work miracles."[8] The movies also teach us the power and strength of family.

"In this life, family is the most precious gift we are given. The most sacred."

-Maria Konstadarou as Yia Yia in *The Sisterhood of the Traveling Pants* (2005)

"Remember, nothing is as strong as family."

–Kevin Clash as Master Splinter in *Teenage Mutant Ninja Turtles* (2014)

---

[6] Russell M. Nelson, "Set in Order Thy House," October 2001 General Conference.

[7] Thomas S. Monson, "Hallmarks of a Happy Home," October 1988 General Conference.

[8] David O. McKay, April 1964 General Conference.

"In the end, Charlie Bucket won a chocolate factory. But Willy Wonka had something even better, a family. And one thing was absolutely certain - life had never been sweeter."

–Geoffrey Holder as Narrator in *Charlie and the Chocolate Factory* (2005)

"Ohana means Family. Family means nobody gets left behind or forgotten."

–Daveigh Chase as Lilo in *Lilo & Stitch* (2002)

"There are all sorts of different families, Katie. But if there's love, dear... those are the ties that bind, and you'll have a family in your heart, forever."

–Robin Williams as Mrs. Doubtfire in *Mrs. Doubtfire* (1993)

"Everyonc has a family. I may not remember their names and what they look like. And I may not even be able to ever find them again, but, um... what were we talking about?"

–Ellen DeGeneres as Dory in *Finding Dory* (2016)

"Now, remember, deputies, the real treasures are your friends and family."

–Tom Hanks as Sheriff Woody in *Toy Story 2* (1999)

"And let me say somethin'. Anybody who's foolish enough to threaten our family, vengeance will be mine!"

–Eddie Murphy as Mushu in *Mulan* (1998)

"I don't ask for much. I don't ask to be rich, and I don't ask to be famous, and I don't ask to play center field for the New York Yankees. I just want to get married and have a wife, and a house, and I want to have a kid, and I want to go see him be a tooth in the school play!"

–Tom Hanks as Allen Bauer in *Splash* (1984)

"There's no place like home. There's no place like home. There's no place like home. There's no place like home."

–Judy Garland as Dorothy Gale in *The Wizard of Oz* (1939)

The Strength of Generations

Today's homelife is important, but can also be seen as part of a much larger panorama of a clan's story, unfolding over the centuries. "Life is a great chain of generations that we in the Church believe must be linked together," taught President Hinckley. "Be faithful. Be true. Be loyal to the great cause of which you are a part. Never become a weak link in the chain of your family's generations."[9] Mulan and her family would appreciate these timeless teachings about honoring a family's heritage. Such connections are also strengthened when attention is paid to both the youngest and oldest in a family.

Walt Disney, for example, would agree with Sister Jean A. Stevens of the Primary General Presidency, who said, "Our Heavenly Father knows children are a key to helping us become

---

[9] Gordon B. Hinckley, "Keep the Chain Unbroken," *BYU Speeches*, 30 November 1999.

like Him. There is so much we can learn from children."[10] And Miss Rhode Island in the Miss Congeniality pageant would agree with Relief Society General President Barbara B. Smith when she said, "We can learn to respect the wisdom, experience, and value of older people. We can strengthen our family ties and appreciate the assets of many generations in a family: the children, youth, adults—including the elderly."[11]

"One weak link can break the chain of a mighty dynasty!"
–Patrick Stewart as Seti in *The Prince of Egypt* (1998)

"We've passed on all we know. A thousand generations live in you now. But this is your fight."
–Mark Hamill as Luke Skywalker in *Star Wars: Episode IX - The Rise of Skywalker* (2019)

"Ancestors, hear my plea, help me not to make a fool of me and to not uproot my family tree."
–Ming-Na Wen as Fa Mulan in *Mulan* (1998)

"We can all learn from our older generations. I remember I learned a lot from my grandmother."
–Heather Burns as Cheryl Frasier in *Miss Congeniality 2* (2005)

---

[10] Jean A. Stevens, "Becomes as a Little Child," April 2011 General Conference.
[11] Barbara B. Smith, "In the Time of Old Age," April 1978 General Conference.

"You can do it. You can do anything. You're the world's greatest grandma."

–Abby Ryder Fortson as Cassie Lang in *Ant-Man and the Wasp* (2018)

"There's no greater joy than that seen through the eyes of a child, and there's a little bit of a child in all of us."

–Tom Hanks as Walt Disney in *Saving Mr. Banks* (2013)

"There's nothing stronger than the bond of family."

–Vin Diesel as Dominic Toretto in *Fast & Furious 4* (2009)

Christlike Friendship

Jesus was a true friend to not only His disciples, but is still a treasured friend to us all. The Lord would have us be kind, inclusive, and friendly. These precious relationships are essential in getting through the ups and downs of this life. "Friendship is a fundamental need of our world," taught Elder Marlin K. Jensen of the Seventy. "The power is in each one of us to be a friend. Old and young, rich and poor, educated and humble, in every language and country, we all have the capacity to be a friend," he said.[12]

---

[12] Marlin K. Jensen, "Friendship: A Gospel Principle," April 1999 General Conference.

The movies are filled with great friendships–from sidekicks and gal pals, to bromance and adventure buddies. "All of us need true friends to love us, to listen to us, to show us the way," admonished President Henry B. Eyring. "You must be such a true friend."[13] Great examples of these include Goose and Maverick in *Top Gun*; Harry, Ron, and Hermione in *Harry Potter*; Sam and Frodo in *The Lord of the Rings*; Timon and Pumbaa in *The Lion King*; Han Solo and Chewbacca in *Star Wars*; Bill and Ted in their *Excellent Adventure*; and Tibby, Lena, Carmen, and Bridget in *The Sisterhood of the Traveling Pants*.

"No man is a failure who has friends."

–Henry Travers as Clarence in *It's a Wonderful Life* (1946)

"I found out what the secret to life is: friends. Best friends."

–Jessica Tandy as Ninny Threadgoode in *Fried Green Tomatoes* (1991)

"That's a lucky lad. There's no greater gift than friendship."

–Tom Hanks as Polar Express Conductor in *The Polar Express* (2004)

"One reality that is inescapable is that there is nothing more valuable than a friend. More than food, more than shelter, and more than weaponry, an ally can save your life."

–Liam Neeson as Qui-Gon Jinn in *Star Wars: Episode I - The Phantom Menace* (1999)

---

[13] Henry B. Eyring, "True Friends," April 2002 General Conference.

"You and I are a team. Nothing is more important than our friendship."

–Billy Crystal as Mike Wazowski in *Monsters, Inc.* (2001)

"I don't have friends. I got family."

–Vin Diesel as Dominic Toretto in *Fast & Furious 7* (2015)

"A day may come when the courage of men fails, when we forsake our friends, and break all bonds of fellowship. But it is not this day."

–Viggo Mortensen as Aragorn in *The Lord of the Rings: The Return of the King* (2003)

"When I'm with you, I don't feel so alone."

–Tate Donovan as Hercules in *Hercules* (1997)

(Directed at Voldemort) "You're the weak one. And you'll never know love, or friendship. And I feel sorry for you."

–Daniel Radcliffe as Harry Potter in *Harry Potter and the Order of the Phoenix* (2007)

"Now Woody, he's been my pal for as long as I can remember. He's brave, like a cowboy should be. And kind, and smart. But the thing that makes Woody special, is he'll never give up on you... ever. He'll be there for you, no matter what."

–John Morris as Andy in *Toy Story 3* (2010)

"Come on, Mr. Frodo. I can't carry it for you... but I can carry you!"

–Sean Astin as Samwise Gamgee in *The Lord of the Rings: The Return of the King* (2003)

"Remember what I told you: do you ever feel lost? Just look into the eyes of the people that you love."

–Chris Pratt as Peter Quill in *Thor: Love and Thunder* (2022)

"Friendship is born at that moment when one person says to another, 'What! You too? I thought I was the only one.'"

–Anthony Hopkins as C.S. Lewis in *Shadowlands* (1993)

"In the event I don't make it back, I want you to know you've been a real friend, R2. My best one, in fact."

–Anthony Daniels as C-3PO in *Star Wars: Episode IX - The Rise of Skywalker* (2019)

"Louis, I think this is the beginning of a beautiful friendship."

–Humphrey Bogart as Rick in *Casablanca* (1942)

Love Thy Neighbor

From the story of the Good Samaritan to the Beatitudes, Jesus taught us to be loving and neighborly to all in this world. When asked "Who is my neighbor?" he gave as broad an answer as his audience could grasp. His apostles have also encouraged us to view the family of man as one. “The children of God have more in common than they have differences,” said President Eyring.[14] We all interact with each other as brothers, sisters, and neighbors. Elder Maxwell rightly said, “no human circle is so small that it does not touch another, and another.”[15] Hollywood often preaches such expansive inclusivity, too.

“We are all connected to each other, in a circle, in a hoop that never ends.”

–Irene Bedard as Pocahontas in *Pocahontas* (1995)

“Sometimes we only see how people are different. But if we look hard enough, you can see how much we're all alike.”

–Linda Larkin as Jasmine in *Aladdin* (1992)

“Now, more than ever, the illusions of division threaten our very existence...We all know the truth: more connects us than separates us. But in times of crisis the wise build bridges, while the foolish build barriers. We must find a way to look after one another, as if we were one single tribe."

–Chadwick Boseman as T' Challa in *Black Panther* (2018)

“No matter how different a Who may appear, he will always be welcomed with holiday cheer.”

–Taylor Momsen as Cindy Lou Who in *How the Grinch Stole Christmas* (2000)

---

[14] Henry B. Eyring, “Our Hearts Knit as One,” October 2008 General Conference.

[15] Neal A. Maxwell, “Notwithstanding My Weakness,” October 1976 General Conference.

"Love thy neighbor — and if he happens to be tall, debonair, and devastating, it will be that much easier."

–Mae West as Flower Belle Lee in *My Little Chickadee* (1940)

"I've always wanted to have a neighbor just like you. . . Won't you be my neighbor? Won't you please, won't you please? Please won't you be my neighbor? Hello neighbor. So good to see you again today."

–Tom Hanks as Mr. Rogers in *A Beautiful Day in the Neighborhood* (2019)

"If everybody got somebody by the hand, maybe everyone could learn and understand."

–Samuel E. Wright a Sebastian in *The Little Mermaid* (1989)

"You measure yourself by the people who measure themselves by you."

–Morgan Freeman as Carter Chambers in *Bucket List* (2007)

Teamwork

"One way you can measure your value in the kingdom of God is to ask, 'How well am I doing in helping others reach their potential?'" said Elder Wirthlin.[16] Connecting with others, helping each other out, is all part of the Father's plan. "Every

---

[16] Joseph B. Wirthlin, "The Virtue of Kindness," April 2005 General Conference.

human soul has the need to feel a part of something," acknowledged Young Women General President Bonnie H. Cordon. "We all want to feel accepted and a part of something bigger than ourselves," she said.[17] We do that when we are part of a team.

The scriptures have great examples of teams (Helaman's stripling warriors, the missionary sons of King Mosiah, the disciples of Jesus of Nazareth, etc.), and so do the movies (the X-men, the Fellowship of the Ring, Ocean's eleven, the Magnificent Seven, the Ghostbusters, and more). These teams all show that "when women and men work together, we accomplish a great deal more than we do working separately," as Sister Jean B. Bingham, Relief Society General President, put it.[18]

"Together we will always rise."

–Chadwick Boseman as T'Challa in *Black Panther* (2018)

"We all get to the peak together, or we don't get there at all."

–Kevin Costner as Al Harrison in *Hidden Figures* (2016)

"Only one is a wanderer; two together are always going somewhere."

–Kim Novak as Madeleine Elster/Judy Barton in *Vertigo* (1958)

---

[17] Bonnie H. Cordon, "Beloved Daughters," *Ensign*, November 2019.

[18] Jean B. Bingham, "United in Accomplishing God's Work," April 2020 General Conference.

"If we don't act together then we are nothing. If we don't stick together we are nothing. And if we can't even trust each other, then we are nothing."

–Christian Bale as Jack Kelly in *Newsies* (1992)

"There are no strangers among those who seek God's mercy."

–Charlton Heston as Moses in *The Ten Commandments* (1965)

"We do things as a team, gentlemen."

–Ed Harris as Coach Jones in *Radio* (2003)

"For the strength of the pack is the wolf, and the strength of the wolf is the pack."

–Bruce Reitherman as Mowgli in *The Jungle Book* (1967)

"I have faith in my team."

–Michael Jordan as Michael Jordan in *Space Jam* (1996)

"We had each other. That's how we won."

–Billy Dee Williams as Lando Calrissian in *Star Wars: Episode IX - The Rise of Skywalker* (2019)

"You have the chance to become part of something much bigger than yourself."

–Patrick Stewart as Professor X in *X-Men: First Class* (2011)

"We look out for our own kind. When all is said and done, we're all we've got."

–Brian Dennehy as Django the Rat in *Ratatouille* (2007)

"In a way, America's like a big ship. And when we all work together and respect each other, that's when the ship gets safely home."

–Heather Burns as Cheryl Frasier in *Miss Congeniality* (2000)

"Remember, son, a house divided against itself cannot stand."

–Hank Azaria as Abraham Lincoln in *Night at the Museum: Battle of the Smithsonian* (2009)

"The only way to get through it is we all work together as a team."

–Michael Caine as Charlie Croker in *The Italian Job* (1969)

"We...are Groot."

–Vin Diesel as Groot in *Guardians of the Galaxy* (2014)

9

KINDNESS & SERVICE

The teachings of Jesus Christ and His servants are replete with admonitions to serve each other, bear one another's burdens, be merciful and filled with charity towards others. "The needs of others are ever present," taught President Monson, "and each of us can do something to help someone."[1] Our compassion and kindness can come through to others in both words and deeds. "How we treat each other really matters!" declared President Nelson. "How we speak to and about others at home, at church, at work, and online really matters," he said.[2]

Speaking Kind Words

Wizards and apostles alike have taught us the power of words–for good and for ill. "The voice that bears profound testimony, utters fervent prayer, and sings the hymns of Zion can be the same voice that berates and criticizes, embarrasses and demeans, inflicts pain and destroys the spirit of oneself and of others in the process," said Elder Holland. "Our words, like our deeds, should be filled with faith and hope and charity."[3]

We sing the hymn "Let us oft speak kind words to each other" and are taught that how we speak to others can bring the spirit of Christ or the spirit of contention. "Look for the good in those about you, and emphasize that good," taught President Hinckley. "Never go around gossiping about your associates or speaking unkind words concerning them. Such words will only

---

[1] Thomas S. Monson, "What Have I Done for Someone Today?" October 2009 General Conference.

[2] Russell M. Nelson, "Peacemakers Needed," April 2023 General Conference.

[3] Jeffery R. Holland, "The Tongue of Angels," April 2007 General Conference.

backfire to hurt you."[4] Animated rabbits and spiders also encourage us to speak kind words.

"If you can't say somethin' nice, don't say nothin' at all."

–Sam Edwards as Thumper in *Bambi* (1942)

"Calling somebody else fat won't make you any skinnier. Calling someone stupid doesn't make you any smarter."

–Lindsay Lohan as Cady Heron in *Mean Girls* (2004)

"And rather than sit here and have a belligerent confrontation with you, 'cause I am a God-fearing man, I'ma do like Jesus H. Christ would do in a situation such as such, and I'm gonna turn the other cheek."

–Marlon Wayans as Buster in *Norbit* (2007)

"If you love someone you say it, you say it right then, out loud. Otherwise the moment just...passes you by."

–Dermot Mulroney as Michael in *My Best Friend's Wedding* (1997)

"Words are, in my not-so-humble opinion, our most inexhaustible source of magic. Capable of both inflicting injury, and remedying it."

–Michael Gambon as Albus Dumbledore in *Harry Potter and the Deathly Hollows: Part 1* (2010)

---

[4] Gordon B. Hinkley, "Stand True and Faithful," April 1996 General Conference.

"With the right words, you can change the world."
–Julia Roberts as Charlotte in *Charlotte's Web* (2006)

Acts of Kindness

There is power in a simple act of kindness. "So often, our acts of service consist of simple encouragement or of giving mundane help with mundane tasks," said President Kimball, "but what glorious consequences can flow from mundane acts and from small but deliberate deeds!"[5] A small act of generosity or selfless assistance to someone can create a positive ripple effect leading to still more goodness. Even the movies teach us that.

"A true selfless act always sparks another."
–J.K. Simmons as Klaus in *Klaus* (2019)

God: "How do we change the world?"
Evan: "One single act of random kindness at a time."
–Morgan Freeman as God, Steve Carrell as Evan Baxter in *Evan Almighty* (2007)

"A hero can be anyone. Even a man doing something as simple and reassuring as putting a coat around a young boy's shoulders to let him know that the world hadn't ended."
–Christian Bale as Bruce Wayne in *The Dark Knight Rises* (2012)

[5] Spencer W. Kimball, "Small Acts of Service," *Ensign,* December 1974.

"It is the small things, everyday deeds of ordinary folk that keeps the darkness at bay. Simple acts of love and kindness."

–Ian McKellen as Gandalf in *The Hobbit: An Unexpected Journey* (2012)

"Deeds will not be less valiant because they are unpraised."

–Viggo Mortensen as Aragorn in *The Lord of the Rings: The Return of the King* (2003)

"So shines a good deed in a weary world."

–Gene Wilder as Willy Wonka as *Willy Wonka & the Chocolate Factory* (1971)

"If you have a choice between being right and being kind, choose kind."

–Mandy Patinkin as Mr. Tushman in *Wonder* (2017)

"Whoever you are, I have always depended on the kindness of strangers."

–Vivien Leigh as Blanche in *A Streetcar Named Desire* (1951)

"Sometimes, when we lose ourselves in fear and despair, in routine and constancy, in hopelessness and tragedy, we can thank God for Bavarian sugar cookies. And, fortunately, when there aren't any cookies, we can still find reassurance in a familiar hand on our skin, or a kind and loving gesture, or subtle encouragement, or a loving embrace or an offer of comfort."

–Emma Thompson as Karen Eiffel in *Stranger Than Fiction* (2006)

Kindness Begins with Me

From the oldest films to new releases, we learn that each of us can demonstrate kindness. From Primary class to General Conference, we have also learned that kindness must come from each of us to change the world for good. "Kindness is the essence of greatness and the fundamental characteristic of the noblest men and women I have known," said Elder Wirthlin. "Kindness is how a Christlike person treats others. Kindness should permeate all of our words and actions at work, at school, at church, and especially in our homes," he said.[6] We are taught in these movie quotes that kindness is always the path to happily ever afters.

"Kindness in heart much better than gold in bank."

–Warner Oland as Charlie Chan in *Charlie Chan in Paris* (1935)

"Be kind. And all will be well."

–Richard Madden as Prince Charming in *Cinderella* (2015)

"If you want to know what a man's like, take a good look at how he treats his inferiors, not his equals."

–Gary Oldman as Sirius Black in *Harry Potter and the Goblet of Fire* (2005)

---

[6] Joseph B. Wirthlin, "The Virtue of Kindness," April 2005 General Conference.

"You is kind. You is smart. You is important."

–Viola Davis as Aibileen Clark in *The Help* (2011)

"When there is kindness, there is goodness. When there is goodness, there is magic."

-Hayley Atwell as Ella's Mother in *Cinderella* (2015)

"Be kind, for everyone is fighting a hard battle. And if you really wanna see what people are, all you have to do is look."

–Jacob Tremblay as Auggie in *Wonder* (2017)

"How little kindness there is in the world today!"

–Sydney Greenstreet as Mr. Peters in *The Mask of Dimitrios* (1944)

"Never underestimate the kindness of the common man, Phillip."

–Kevin Costner as Butch Haynes in *A Perfect World* (1993)

"Auggie can't change how he looks. Maybe we should change how we see."

–Mandy Patinkin as Mr. Tushman in *Wonder* (2017)

"And yet, through it all, Cinderella remained ever gentle and kind."

–Helena Bonham Carter as Fairy Godmother in *Cinderella* (2015)

"Be excellent to each other. And party on, dude!"
–Robert V. Barron as Abraham Lincoln in *Bill & Ted's Excellent Adventure* (1989)

Peace, Courtesy, Civility

The Prince of Peace taught us to put down our weapons of hate, vitriol, and destruction. He showed us that we can disagree better, that we can take the first step to bridging divides, and that we can bring civility and courtesy to our interactions. "Whatsoever ye would that men should do to you, do ye even so to them," the Savior taught with His Golden Rule. "Blessed are the peacemakers," He said.[7] We must stand for goodness and light. "The best is yet to come for those who spend their lives building up others," said President Nelson. "I bless you to replace belligerence with beseeching, animosity with understanding, and contention with peace."[8]

"And I felt His voice take the sword out of my hand."
–Charlton Heston as Judah Ben-Hur in *Ben-Hur* (1959)

"No blades. No bows. Leave your weapons here."
–Andrew Lawden as Sergeant in *Robin Hood: Prince of Thieves* (1991)

---

[7] Matthew 7:12 and Matthew 5:9
[8] Russell M. Nelson, "Peacemakers Needed," April 2023 General Conference.

"Wakanda survived for so long by only fighting when absolutely necessary."

–Danai Gurira as Okoye in *Black Panther* (2018)

"It's not enough to be against something. You have to be for something better."

–Robert Downey Jr. as Tony Stark in *Captain America: Civil War* (2016)

"There are kingly virtues other than bravery. Courtesy is one of them."

–Freddie Jones as Ynyr in *Krull* (1983)

"Life does not treat you fairly or unfairly, it merely is. It is up to each of us to be fair, or unfair."

–Liam Neeson as Qui-Gon Jinn in *Star Wars: Episode I - The Phantom Menace* (1999)

"Someone has to take the first step."

–Daniel Dae Kim as Chief Benja in *Raya and the Last Dragon* (2021)

"Aunt Lucy said: 'If we're kind and polite, the world will be right.'"

–Ben Whishaw as Paddington in *Paddington 2* (2017)

Serving One Another

King Mosiah in the Book of Mormon famously taught, "when ye are in the service of your fellow beings ye are only in the service of your God."[9] We have a duty to serve our fellow beings, and can even lead out on initiating service and love. "We must take the first step," said Elder Scott. "Our initial acts of kindness or service to others provide us with channels of inspiration and power," he said.[10] We must give back and find the joy in putting others before ourselves.

"All creatures of good heart need your help."
–Maria Holvoe as Cherlindrea in *Willow* (1988)

"Serving is the supreme art. God is the first of servants. God serves men, but he's not a servant to men."
–Giustino Durano as Uncle Eliseo (Zio) in *Life is Beautiful* (1997)

"By protecting others, you save yourselves. If you only think of yourself, you'll only destroy yourself."
–Takashi Shimura as Kambei Shimada in *Seven Samurai* (1954)

"While others search for what they can take, a true king searches for what he can give."
–James Earl Jones as Mufasa in *The Lion King* (2019)

---

[9] Mosiah 2:17
[10] Richard G. Scott, "The Power to Make a Difference," October 1983 General Conference.

"Legacy. What is a legacy? It's planting seeds in a garden you never get to see."

–Lin-Manuel Miranda as Alexander Hamilton in *Hamilton* (2020)

"Maleficent doesn't know anything about love or kindness or the joy of helping others. You know, sometimes I think she isn't very happy."

–Barbara Jo Allen as Fauna in *Sleeping Beauty* (1959)

"I guess you already know that there are angels masquerading as people walking around this planet."

–Mary Stuart Masterson as Idgie Threadgoode in *Fried Green Tomatoes* (1991)

"There's good in everyone. There's good in everyone."

–Kevin McCann as Ethical Bug in *Puss in Boots: The Last Wish* (2022)

Compassion & Care

The art of charity is in the caring and compassion for others. "The expression of compassion for others is the essence of the gospel of Jesus Christ," taught Elder Ulisses Soares of the Twelve.[11] The silver screen is filled with examples of heroes who care, who help, and who passionately put others first.

[11] Ulisses Soares, "The Savior's Abiding Compassion," October 2021 General Conference.

President Monson taught as much, too, when he said "the needs of others are ever present, and each of us can do something to help someone."[12]

"I'm here. What do you need?"

–Jonathan Goff as Kristoff in *Frozen 2* (2019)

"But our lives aren't just measured in years. They're measured in the lives of people we touch around us."

–Josh Hutcherson as Peeta Mellark in *Hunger Games: Catching Fire* (2013)

"Look for the helpers. You'll always find people who are helping."

–Tom Hanks as Fred Rogers in *Beautiful Day in the Neighborhood* (2019)

"My church comforts the sick and dying. My church feeds the poor."

–Stellan Skarsgård as Commander Maximillian Richter in *Angels and Demons* (2009)

"Unless someone like you cares a whole awful lot, nothing is going to get better. It's not."

–Danny DeVito as the Lorax in *The Lorax* (2012)

"You're cute when you care."

–Annie Potts as Bo Peep in *Toy Story 2* (1999)

---

[12] Thomas S. Monson, "What Have I Done for Someone Today?" October 2009 General Conference.

"I don't like to see decent people pushed around."

–Edward G. Robinson as Johnny Blake in *Bullets or Ballots* (1936)

"We have to surprise them with compassion, with restraint and generosity."

–Morgan Freeman as Nelson Mandela in *Invictus* (2009)

"You'll find there's room for all of us here."

–Ben Kingsley as Mahatma Gandhi in *Gandhi* (1982)

"You treat a disease, you win, you lose. You treat a person, I guarantee you, you'll win, no matter what the outcome."

–Robin Williams as Dr. Hunter Patch Adams in *Patch Adams* (1998)

10

LOVE ONE ANOTHER

The bedrock of Christianity is love. Jesus taught us to love each other, to love our spouse, our families, our neighbors, and to even love our enemies. "Love one another; as I have loved you, that ye also love one another," the Savior taught. "By this shall all men know that ye are my disciples, if ye have love one to another."[1]

We learn in both gospel study and many blockbuster movies that love is essential to life, that love has unique properties unlike anything else in the universe, that love is powerful, and that love brings couples together in romance and marriage. We learn that we must not only give love, but be willing to accept love. And we even learn that the highest form of love is Godlike charity.

Love is Life

"Life without love is not real life at all," said Sister Smith. "Love is the life-giving force that renews the spirit of men and women and brings a new life to the world."[2] She's right, and from Hogwarts to Middle Earth, wise film characters have pointed out the eternal truth: love *is* life. President Uchtdorf declared that "Love is the measure of our faith," and so if we are to be true to the faith, we have to love. It is the lifeforce of humanity and brings light, richness, and depth to our lives.[3]

---

[1] John 13:34-35
[2] Barbra B. Smith, "Love Is Life," *BYU Speeches,* 14 February 1986.
[3] Dieter F. Uchtdorf, "The Love of God," October 2009 General Conference.

"Do not pity the dead. Pity the living and, above all, those who live without love."

–Michael Gambon as Albus Dumbledore in *Harry Potter and the Deathly Hallows: Part 2* (2011)

"'Life without love is like a tree without blossoms or fruit.' Gibran, Lebanese."

–Mindy Kaling as Mrs. Who in *A Wrinkle in Time* (2018)

"Medicine, law, business, engineering, these are noble pursuits and necessary to sustain life. But poetry, beauty, romance, love, these are what we stay alive for."

–Robin Williams as John Keating in *Dead Poets Society* (1989)

"I'd rather die tomorrow than live a hundred years without knowing you."

–Irene Bedard as Pocahontas in *Pocahontas* (1995)

"I would rather share one lifetime with you than face all the ages of this world alone."

–Liv Tyler as Arwen in *The Lord of the Rings: The Fellowship of the Ring* (2001)

"Our lives are not fully lived if we're not willing to die for those we love, for what we believe."

–David Oyelowo as Martin Luther King Jr. in *Selma* (2014)

"Compassion, which I would define as unconditional love, is essential to a Jedi's life."

–Hayden Christensen as Anakin Skywalker in *Star Wars: Episode II - Attack of the Clones* (2002)

"You know what? We got to have more love, More understanding every day of our lives."

–Sophie Okonedo as Salome Otterbourne in *Death on the Nile* (2022)

"There are only four questions of value in life, Don Octavio. What is sacred? Of what is the spirit made? What is worth living for, and what is worth dying for? The answer to each is the same: only love."

–Johnny Depp as Don Juan DeMarco in *Don Juan DeMarco* (1994)

"We are not defined by where we are from... but by whom we love."

–Tom Bonington as Priest in *Maleficent: Mistress of Evil* (2019)

"People do fall in love. People do belong to each other, because that's the only chance that anyone's got for true happiness."

–George Peppard as Paul Varjak in *Breakfast at Tiffany's* (1961)

"Love is putting someone else's needs before yours."

–Josh Gad as Olaf in *Frozen* (2013)

Unique Properties of Love

Love is neither animal, vegetable, or mineral. It isn't a solid, liquid, or gas. Hollywood points out that you can feel it, it is permanent, it's an ability, and a many-splendored thing. Love makes us want to be our best selves, and they say it is absolutely worth it, even though it often may lead to grief and pain when a loved one is gone. "The only way to avoid the grief would be to not experience the love; and it is love that gives life its richness and meaning," said Elder Lance B. Wickman of the Seventy.[4] Another Seventy, Elder F. Burton Howard, taught that love is unique in that it can grow and change based on how you treat it. "If you want something to last forever, you treat it differently," he said. "It becomes special because you have made it so, and it grows more beautiful and precious as time goes by." Movies have much wisdom to impart on love's unique properties.

"Our love is like the wind… I can't see it, but I sure can feel it."
–Shane West as Landon Carter in *A Walk to Remember* (2002)

"I just thought of one thing that's permanent. Love!"
–Josh Gad as Olaf in *Frozen 2* (2019)

"I'm not a smart man but I know what love is."
–Tom Hanks as Forrest Gump in *Forrest Gump* (1994)

[4] Lance B. Wickman, "But If Not," October 2002 General Conference.

"Do you have any idea how love works? When you love someone, you love them - through all their moods and changes over time. Their worst qualities peak at nuisance. Their flaws become freckles."

–Susannah Fielding as Katherine in *Death on the Nile* (2022)

"Love is not a feeling, Mr. Burns. It's an ability."

–Felipe Dieppa as Marty Barasco in *Dan in Real Life* (2007)

"Why love, if losing hurts so much? I have no answers anymore: only the life I have lived. Twice in that life I've been given the choice: as a boy and as a man. The boy chose safety, the man chooses suffering. The pain now is part of the happiness then. That's the deal."

–Anthony Hopkins as Jack (C.S. Lewis) in *Shadowlands* (1993)

"Between grief and nothing...I'll choose grief."

–Jeffrey Jones as Ed Rooney in *Ferris Bueller's Day Off* (1986)

"You make me want to be a better man."

–Jack Nicholson as Melvin Udall in *As Good as It Gets* (1997)

"To make something special you just have to believe it's special."

–James Hong as Mr. Ping in *Kung Fu Panda* (2008)

"Because when I look at you, I can feel it. And I look at you and I'm home."

–Ellen DeGeneres as Dory in *Finding Nemo* (2003)

"Love is like oxygen! Love is a many-splendored thing. Love lifts us up where we belong. All you need is love!"

–Ewan McGregor as Christian in *Moulin Rouge!* (2001)

Power of Love

President Hinckley once said, "Let love be your lodestar. It is the greatest force on earth."[5] Many messages from the silver screen talk about the power of love. So does the Bible and church leaders. The New Testament tells us that "There is no fear in love; but perfect love casteth out fear."[6] And Elder Wirthlin taught love is so powerful it outlasts all else. "True love lasts forever," he said. "It is eternally patient and forgiving. It believes, hopes, and endures all things."[7] Marty McFly skateboarded to the Huey Lewis and the News song, "The Power of Love," but what do the actor lines say about this tremendous force?

---

[5] Quoted in Grant C. Anderson, "Remember and Act," Seminaries and Institutes of Religion Satellite Broadcast, 4 August 2015.

[6] 1 John 4:18

[7] Joseph B. Wirthlin, "The Great Commandment," October 2007 General Conference.

"That love business is a powerful thing. Greater than gravity? Well, yes. In its way, yes, I'd say it's the greatest force on Earth."

–Karl Swenson as Merlin in *The Sword and the Stone* (1963)

"To have been loved so deeply, even though the person who loved us is gone, will give us some protection forever. It is in your very own skin."

–Richard Harris as Albus Dumbledore in *Harry Potter and the Sorcerer's Stone* (2001)

"Love thaws a frozen heart."

–Josh Gad as Olaf in *Frozen* (2013)

"Love is bigger than any tidal wave or fear."

–AnnaSophia Robb as Bethany Hamilton in *Soul Surfer* (2011)

"Whenever I despair, I remember that the way of truth and love has always won. There may be tyrants and murderers, and for a time, they may seem invincible, but in the end, they always fail. Think of it: always."

–Ben Kingsley as Gandhi in *Gandhi* (1982)

"Everything's going to be alright, because I love you very much."

–Christian Bale as Alfred Borden in *The Prestige* (2006)

"It is love that will heal you. It's what heals us all."
–Michelle Pfeiffer as Queen Ingrith in *Maleficent: Mistress of Evil* (2019)

"Love is an open door."
–Kristen Bell as Princess Anna in *Frozen* (2013)

"Sonny, true love is the greatest thing in the world… except for a nice MLT. Mutton, lettuce, and tomato sandwich, where the mutton is nice and lean and the tomatoes are ripe. (smacks his lips) They're so perky; I love that."
–Billy Crystal as Miracle Max in *The Princess Bride* (1987)

"Only love can save this world."
–Gal Gadot as Diana Prince in *Wonder Woman* (2017)

Romance & Marriage

It is estimated that nearly 76,000 romance movies have been made in the past century, so we have plenty of quotes from films about the romantic aspect of love. Such love is an important part of the gospel plan, too, especially when leading to marriage and family creation. Elder F. Melvin Hammon of the Seventy summarized well decades of teachings from church leaders when he spoke to students at BYU. He said to the men: "I encourage you to date, find a girl that will assist you in honoring your priesthood covenants, marry her in the temple, have beautiful babies, and begin the lifelong journey of becoming a family together forever."[8]

President Boyd K. Packer once told this same group, "You are old enough now to fall in love—not the puppy love of the elementary years, not the confused love of the teens, but the full-blown love of eligible men and women, newly matured, ready for life," he said enthusiastically. "I mean romantic love, with all the full intense meaning of the word, with all of the power and turbulence and frustration, the yearning, the restraining, and all of the peace and beauty and sublimity of love. No experience can be more beautiful, no power more compelling, more exquisite," he said.[9] So let's enjoy a few choice movie quotes about this exquisite form of love!

"You need to find yourself a girl, mate."

–Johnny Depp as Jack Sparrow in *Pirates of the Caribbean: The Curse of the Black Pearl* (2003)

"Let me reiterate what Brigham Young said: if you're 25 years old and unmarried, you're a menace to society. Just something for everybody to ponder."

–Steve Young as Brother Niner in *The Singles Ward* (2002)

"Some people are worth melting for."

–Josh Gad as Olaf in *Frozen* (2013)

---

[8] F. Melvin Hammond, "The Vision of Eternity," *BYU Speeches,* 11 February 2003.

[9] Boyd K. Packer, "The Search for Eternal Love," *BYU Speeches,* 3 November 1963.

"It cannot have escaped your notice that for some time past the friendship I have felt for you has ripened into a deeper feeling, a feeling more beautiful, more pure, more sacred. Dare I name it? Can it be love?"

–Clark Gable as Rhett Butler in *Gone with the Wind* (1939)

"I want to tell you with my remaining strength that I love you. I always have. I'll drift next to you every day as a ghost just to be with you. Even if I was banished to the darkest place, my love will keep me from being a lonely spirit."

–Chow Yun-Fat as Li Mu Bai in *Crouching Tiger, Hidden Dragon* (2000)

"You were my new dream."

–Zachary Levi as Flynn Rider in *Tangled* (2010)

"I'm George, George McFly, and I'm your density. I mean, I'm your destiny."

–Crispin Glover as George McFly in *Back to the Future* (1985)

"Don't forget: I'm also just a girl, standing in front of a boy, asking him to love her."

–Julia Roberts as Anna Scott in *Notting Hill* (1999)

"So it's not gonna be easy. It's gonna be really hard, and we're gonna have to work at this every day. But I wanna do that because I want you. I want all of you, forever. You and me. Every day."

–Ryan Gosling as Noah in *The Notebook* (2004)

"You have bewitched me, body and soul, and I love, I love, I love you. I never wish to be parted from you from this day on."

–Matthew Macfadyen as Mr. Darcy in *Pride & Prejudice* (2005)

"Love that fierce doesn't vanish. I love him. I love him madly. Badly, at every minute. It's not something I can switch off. There's a reason the heart is the organ given to love, you know. If it stops to rest, we die."

–Emma Mackey as Jacqueline de Bellefort in *Death on the Nile* (2022)

"I've come here with no expectations, only to profess, now that I am at liberty to do so, that my heart is, and always will be, yours."

–Hugh Grant as Edward Ferrars in *Sense and Sensibility* (1995)

"When I first saw you, I felt like I knew you, and I couldn't stop seeing my life with you, and building a family together. One that isn't stuck in the pain of the past. It's very pretty. And so, if you're asking me if my proposition still stands, then my answer is yes. Yes. A thousand times, yes."

–Isabel Graysmark as Alicia Vikander in *The Light Between Oceans* (2016)

"A man must marry where his heart leads him, little mother."

–Victor Mature as Samson in *Samson and Delilah* (1949)

"Listen, sugar, the only way that you can keep me warm is to wrap me up in a marriage license."

–Gloria Grahame as Angel in *The Greatest Show on Earth* (1952)

"Mawage. Mawage is wot bwings us together today. Mawage, that blessed awangement, that dweam wifin a dweam. And wuv, tru wuv, will fowow you foweva. So tweasure your wuv."

–Peter Cook as The Impressive Clergyman in *The Princess Bride* (1987)

"I vow to fiercely love you in all your forms, now and forever. I promise to never forget that this is a once in a lifetime love."

–Channing Tatum as Leo in *The Vow* (2012)

"You can't have a happy married life if you're always suspicious. No. There can't be any doubts in marriage. Marriage is based on faith and if you've lost that, you've lost everything."

–Cary Grant as Jerry Warriner in *The Awful Truth* (1937)

"This is true love - you think this happens every day?"

–Cary Elwes as Westley in *The Princess Bride* (1987)

"It was a million tiny little things that, when you added them all up, they meant we were supposed to be together, and I knew it. I knew it the first time I touched her. It was like coming home, only to no home I'd ever known. I was just taking her hand to help her out of a car and I knew it. It was like magic."

–Tom Hanks as Sam Baldwin in *Sleepless in Seattle* (1993)

Accepting Love

You are loved by more people than you may realize. "I hope you know how much you are loved by your family, your Primary teachers, and, most importantly, by Heavenly Father and Jesus Christ," said Primary General President Coleen K. Menlove to the child in all of us.[10] It is critical in life's path to both give love and be willing to accept love. Love works best when it is a two-way proposition.

"Just take a minute and think about all the people who loved us into being."

–Tom Hanks as Fred Rogers in *A Beautiful Day in the Neighborhood* (2019)

"We accept the love we think we deserve."

–Logan Lerman as Charlie in *The Perks of Being a Wallflower* (2012)

---

[10] Coleen K. Menlove, "All Thy Children Shall Be Taught," April 2005 General Conference.

"For here you are, standing there, loving me; whether or not you should."

–Julie Andrews as Maria in *The Sound of Music* (1965)

"And remember, my sentimental friend, that a heart is not judged by how much *you* love; but by how much you are loved by others."

–Frank Morgan as The Wizard of Oz in *The Wizard of Oz* (1939)

"In my opinion, the best thing you can do is find someone who loves you for exactly what you are. Good mood, bad mood, ugly, pretty, handsome, what have you."

–J.K. Simmons as Mac MacGuff in *Juno* (2007)

"The greatest thing you'll ever learn is just to love and be loved in return."

–Ewan McGregor as Christian in *Moulin Rouge!* (2001)

"Does someone need a hug?"

–Will Ferrell as Buddy the Elf in *Elf* (2003)

God's Love

There is no greater love than God's. Our Heavenly Parents love us purely for who we are and with the full-blown love of charity. They love us no matter what, and even love us so much that they will not force us to love them back. "Though God loves us perfectly, He will not force us to love Him in return," pointed out Elder H. Ross Workman of the Seventy. "We are invited to 'abide' in His love (see John 15:10), but we must freely choose to do so," he said.[11] Godlike love is to love our enemies, to be charitable and generous, and to be purely unselfish. "True love blooms when we care more about another person than we care about ourselves," said Elder Holland.[12]

"There are so many things I don't know. But I know God loves you."

–Jennifer Garner as Christy Beam in *Miracles from Heaven* (2016)

"Love is always patient and kind. It is never jealous. Love is never boastful or conceited. It is never rude or selfish. It does not take offense and is not resentful."

–Shane West as Landon Carter in *A Walk to Remember* (2002)

"I know there is a law in life, that blood gets more blood as dog begets dog. Death generates death, as the vulture breeds the vulture! But the voice I heard today on the hill said, 'Love your enemy. Do good to those who despitefully use you.'"

–Haya Harareet as Esther in *Ben-Hur* (1959)

"I love you without knowing how, why, or even from where."

–Robin Williams as Patch Adams in *Patch Adams* (1998)

---

[11] H. Ross Workman, "Safely Anchored by Love," *Ensign*, December 2003.
[12] Jeffrey R. Holland, "How Do I Love Thee?" *BYU Speeches*, 15 February 2000.

Bruce: "How do you make someone love you without changing free will?"
God: "Welcome to my world."

–Jim Carrey as Bruce and Morgan Freeman as God in *Bruce Almighty* (2003)

"My name is Dug. I have just met you and I love you."

–Bob Peterson as Dug in *Up* (2009)

"When we love someone we are really loving God."

–Victor Williams as Rev. Henry Biggs in *The Preacher's Wife* (1996)

"To love another person is to see the face of God."

–Hugh Jackman as Jean Valjean in *Les Misérables* (2012)

II

HAPPINESS & JOY

The covenant path is also called the "great plan of happiness,"[1] and finding happiness and joy in this life is a significant part of God's plan for His children here on Earth. "Men are that they might have joy," declared the Prophet Nephi[2]. "Consider on the blessed and happy state of those that keep the commandments of God," pointed out King Benjamin.[3] "A merry heart doeth good like a medicine," advised the writer of Proverbs.[4] The movies can also be a place to find happiness and to learn how to find joy.

Pursuing Happiness

Prophets and apostles, as well as a number of classic films, advise us to pursue happiness and take responsibility for our own attitudes of joy. "So much of your happiness is in your hands, not in events or circumstances or fortune or misfortune," taught Elder Holland.[5] "External circumstances don't really matter or determine our happiness," agreed President Uchtdorf. "We do matter. We determine our happiness. You and I are ultimately in charge of our own happiness," he said.[6] President Nelson likewise has taught of the peace we can find in overcoming the world and focusing instead on our Savior. "The

---

[1] Alma 42:8
[2] 2 Nephi 2:25
[3] Mosiah 2:41
[4] Proverbs 17:22
[5] Jeffrey R. Holland, "The Gospel Path to Happiness," *Ensign*, September 2017.
[6] Dieter F. Uchtdorf, "Of Regrets and Resolutions." October 2012 General Conference.

joy we feel has little to do with the circumstances of our lives and everything to do with the focus of our lives," he said.[7]

"Think of all the joy you'll find when you leave the world behind and bid your cares goodbye."

–The Mellowmen Quartet in *Peter Pan* (1953)

"There comes a day when you're gonna look around and realize happiness is where you are."

–Christopher Jackson as Chief Tui in *Moana* (2016)

"It is not the destination so much as the journey, they say."

–Johnny Depp as Jack Sparrow in *Pirates of the Caribbean: On Stranger Tides* (2011)

"The journey is what brings us happiness not the destination."

–Scott Mechlowicz as Dan Millman in *Peaceful Warrior* (2006)

"It was right then that I started thinking about Thomas Jefferson on the Declaration of Independence and the part about our right to life, liberty, and the pursuit of happiness. And I remember thinking how did he know to put the pursuit part in there? That maybe happiness is something that we can only pursue and maybe we can actually never have it. No matter what. How did he know that?"

–Will Smith as Christopher Gardner in *The Pursuit of Happyness* (2006)

---

[7] Russell M. Nelson, "Joy and Spiritual Survival," October 2016 General Conference.

"The key to a happy life is to accept you are never actually in control [of everything]."

–Simon Masrani as Irrfan Khan in *Jurassic World* (2015)

"You're out of the woods, you're out of the dark, you're out of the night. Step into the sun, step into the light."

–Optimistic Voices in *The Wizard of Oz* (1939)

"May the odds be ever in your favor."

–Elizabeth Banks as Effie in *The Hunger Games* (2012)

What Brings Happiness

President Uchtdorf once taught, "We were created with the express purpose and potential of experiencing a fulness of joy."[8] Sometimes such simple joys come through experiencing some of the basic fun activities of life. "We are to learn how to enjoy the things of life," said Brigham Young, encouraging "wholesome recreation" such as singing, dancing, attending the theater, playing ball, running, and more.[9] Movies also point out the happiness that comes from keeping things simple, running, wit and humor, dancing, good food, beautiful things, even getting one's hair brushed and more!

---

[8] Dieter F. Uchtdorf, "Happiness, Your Heritage," October 2008 General Conference.

[9] *Discourses of Brigham Young*, Selected by John A. Widtsoe, 1941, p. 237.

"Why do you always complicate things that are really quite simple?"

–Julie Andrews as Mary Poppins in *Mary Poppins* (1964)

"I believe God made me for a purpose, but he also made me fast. And when I run I feel His pleasure."

–Ian Charleson as Eric Liddell in *Chariots of Fire* (1981)

"Wit beyond measure is man's greatest treasure."

–Evanna Lynch as Luna Lovegood in *Harry Potter and the Order of the Phoenix* (2007)

"There are two types of beings in the universe, those who dance, and those who do not."

–Dave Bautista as Drax in *Guardians of the Galaxy: Volume 2* (2017)

"Don't miss out on the joys of life. Like, uh, Pizza."

–Jamie Foxx as Joe in *Soul* (2020)

"One of the great joys in life is having one's hair brushed."

–Vanessa Redgrave as Claire in *Letters to Juliet* (2010)

"Now, think of the happiest things. It's the same as having wings."

–Bobby Driscoll as Peter Pan in *Peter Pan* (1953)

Larry Daley: "You know how you were telling me that the key to happiness was something but then the sun came up? I think I figured it out. It's doing what you love."
Teddy Roosevelt: "I was going to say diet and exercise, but the love thing's good too."

–Ben Stiller as Larry Daley and Robin Williams as Teddy Roosevelt in *Night at the Museum: Battle of the Smithsonian* (2009)

"Exercise gives you endorphins. Endorphins make you happy. Happy people just don't shoot their husbands. They just don't!"

–Reese Witherspoon as Elle Woods in *Legally Blonde* (2001)

"You didn't know what a good thing you had when you had it."

–Una Merkel as Verbena 'Ever's Housekeeper' in *The Parent Trap* (1961)

"I remember one morning getting up at dawn, there was such a sense of possibility. You know, that feeling? And I remember thinking to myself: So, this is the beginning of happiness. This is where it starts. And of course there will always be more. It never occurred to me it wasn't the beginning. It was happiness. It was the moment. Right then."

–Meryl Streep as Clarissa Vaughn in *The Hours* (2002)

"A thing of beauty is a joy forever."

–Julie Andrews as Mary Poppins in *Mary Poppins* (1964)

Celebrating Happiness

Prophets, apostles, and the Bible itself remind us to smile, laugh, and have a merry heart. "The next time you're tempted to groan, you might try to laugh instead," advised Elder Wirthlin. "It will extend your life and make the lives of all those around you more enjoyable," he said.[10] How much better is it to laugh than to cry? The advice to be cheerful is solid, coming from leaders who lived nearly a century. "In all of living have much of fun and laughter," said a smiling President Hinckley. "Life is to be enjoyed, not just endured."[11] Loving life, cheerfully celebrating the good times, is an important gospel principle. Reminders to smile, laugh, and cheer abound in films, too.

"A laugh can be a very powerful thing. Why, sometimes in life, it's the only weapon we have."

–Charles Fleischer as Roger Rabbit in *Who Framed Roger Rabbit?* (1998)

"Remember, laughter is ten times more powerful than screams."

–Billy Crystal as Mike Wazowski in *Monsters, Inc.* (2001)

"A little nonsense now and then is cherished by the wisest men."

–Gene Wilder as Willy Wonka in *Willy Wonka and the Chocolate Factory* (1971)

---

[10] Joseph B. Wirthlin, "Come What May, and Love It," October 2008 General Conference.

[11] Gordon B. Hinckley, "Stand True and Faithful," April 1996 General Conference.

"I'm the king of the world!"

–Leonardo DiCaprio as Jack Dawson in *Titanic* (1997)

"Yahoo!"

–Harrison Ford as Han Solo in *Star Wars: Episode IV: A New Hope* (1977)

"I love you, Joy. I love you so much. You made me so happy. I didn't know I could be so happy."

–Anthony Hopkins as Jack (C.S. Lewis) in *Shadowlands* (1993)

"This is a nice moment, let's not ruin it."

–Tom Cruise as Maverick in *Top Gun: Maverick* (2022)

Joy Amidst Trials

Despite our pursuit of happiness in life, it doesn't mean every day is sunshine and rainbows. "I do not think God in his glory or the angels of heaven or the prophets on earth intend to make us happy all the time, every day in every way, given the testing and trial this earthly realm is intended to provide," counseled Elder Holland.[12] And it's true. Even as we strive to live after the manner of happiness, we will have our emotional highs and lows. And that's OK. "When we open up about our emotional challenges, admitting we are not perfect, we give others

[12] Jeffrey R. Holland, "The Quest Happiness," *Ensign*, September 2016.

permission to share their struggles," said Sister Reyna I. Aburto of the Relief Society General Presidency.[13] The movies have some great lines about not always being happy, about the reality of our feelings, and tips on how to cheer up and turn back on the light!

"Oh, Joy, where are you?"

–Bill Hader as Fear in *Inside Out* (2015)

"Being happy is great, but you don't have to be happy all the time. A little bit of sadness sometimes makes your life more colorful."

–Phyllis Smith as Sadness in *Inside Out* (2015)

"You feel what you feel and your feelings are real."

–Jonanthan Goff as Kristoff in *Frozen 2* (2019)

"It is alright to cry."

–Scott Adsit as Baymax in *Big Hero 6* (2014)

"We can't have the happiness of yesterday without the pain of today. That's the deal."

–Debra Winger as Joy Gresham in *Shadowlands* (1993)

"Being happy isn't having everything in your life be perfect. Maybe it's about stringing together all the little things."

–Jenna Boyd as Bailey in *The Sisterhood of the Traveling Pants* (2005)

---

[13] Reyna I. Aburto, "Thru Cloud and Sunshine, Lord, Abide with Me!" October 2019 General Conference.

"When I'm feeling sad, I simply remember my favorite things, and then I don't feel so bad."

–Julie Andrews as Maria in *The Sound of Music* (1965)

"We are trying to give the world positive ways of dealing with their feelings."

–Tom Hanks as Fred Rogers in *A Beautiful Day in the Neighborhood* (2019)

"What do you do when things go wrong? Oh! You sing a song!"

–Adriana Caselotti as Snow White in *Snow White and the Seven Dwarfs* (1937)

"Happiness can be found, even in the darkest of times, if one only remembers to turn on the light."

–Michael Gambon as Albus Dumbledore in *Harry Potter and the Prisoner of Azkaban* (2004)

"We must face tomorrow, whatever it may hold, with determination, joy and bravery."

–Dustin Hoffman as Edward Magorium in *Mr. Magorium's Wonder Emporium* (2007)

Bringing Joy to Others

We have a duty to lift others, to share joy, and to spread goodwill in this world. "Be happy. Wear a smile. Have fun,"[14] encouraged President Hinckley. We all have gifts and talents we can use to make the world a better place. "Take opportunities to develop these divine gifts and then use them to bless others," taught Sister Margaret D. Nadauld, Young Women General President. "Be happy. Scatter a little sunshine."[15]

"I can only do good, dear, to bring joy and happiness."
–Barbara Jo Allen as Fauna in *Sleeping Beauty* (1959)

"Remember, you're the one who can fill the world with sunshine."
–Adriana Caselotti as Snow White in *Snow White and the Seven Dwarfs* (1937)

"Smile—it increases your face value."
–Dolly Parton as Truvy in *Steel Magnolias* (1989)

"Smile, my boy. It's sunrise."
–Robin Williams as Teddy Roosevelt in *Night at the Museum: Secret of the Tomb* (2014)

---

[14] Gordon B. Hinckley, "How Can I Become the Woman of Whom I Dream?" *New Era,* November 2001.
[15] Margaret D. Nadauld, "Turning Hearts to the Family," April 1998 General Conference.

"Smilers wear a crown, losers wear a frown."
–Michael Caine as Victor Melling in *Miss Congeniality* (2000)

"I just like to smile. Smiling's my favorite."
–Will Ferrell as Buddy the Elf in *Elf* (2003)

"You know, the ancient Egyptians had a beautiful belief about death. When their souls got to the entrance to heaven, the guards asked two questions. Their answers determined whether they were able to enter or not. 'Have you found joy in your life?' 'Has your life brought joy to others?'"
–Morgan Freeman as Carter Chambers in *The Bucket List* (2007)

12

INDIVIDUAL WORTH

For many years, one of the Young Women values was "Individual Worth." Scripture, prophets, and many films also taught us that everyone is special and that individually we are all unique and of great worth. We are told to believe in ourselves, and be loyal to who we really are. We are also reminded of the beauty inside of each of us as children of a Heavenly King and that we should always be loyal to that essence. Or as President Lee said, "be loyal to the royal within you."[1]

Everyone is Special

"Remember the worth of souls is great in the sight of God," the scriptures say.[2] We are all children of Heavenly Parents and our souls have a tremendous past, a special role in this life, and a bright eternal future. Elder Clark G. Gilbert of the Seventy taught, "We believe in the divine potential of all of God's children and in our ability to become something more in Christ."[3] We are all dear to our Creator, and part of that proof is the blessing of our individual bodies. President Nelson reminded us that everyone has this gift. "A unique body is given to each of us by our loving Heavenly Father," he said.[4] Every individual on this planet is a valued brother and sister, and many films point out the inherent worth of all.

---

[1] Harold B. Lee, "Be Loyal to the Royal Within You," *BYU Speeches*, 11 September 1973.

[2] D&C 18:10

[3] Clark. G. Gilbert, "Becoming More in Christ: The Parable of the Slope," October 2021 General Conference.

[4] Russell M. Nelson, "Your Body: A Magnificent Gift to Cherish," *New Era*, August 2019.

"I am something - everyone is."

–Sidney Poitier as Mark Thackery in *To Sir, with Love* (1967)

"Everybody is somebody. Even a nobody."

–John Kani as Rafiki in *The Lion King* (2019)

"You are capable of amazing things. Because you are the Special. And so am I. And so is everyone."

–Chris Pratt as Emmett in *The LEGO Movie* (2014)

"Machines never come with any extra parts, you know. They always come with the exact amount they need. So, I figured that if the entire world was one big machine, I couldn't be an extra part. I had to be here for some reason."

–Asa Butterfield as Hugo Cabret in *Hugo* (2011)

"Everyone is born, but not everyone is born the same. One way or another, every human being is unique, for better or for worse."

–Danny DeVito as Narrator in *Matilda* (1996)

"After all, the wool from the black sheep is just as warm."

–Anna Lee as Sister Margaretta in *The Sound of Music* (1965)

"There's room for everyone on the Nice List."

–Will Ferrell as Buddy the Elf in *Elf* (2003)

"We're all human, aren't we? Every human life is worth the same, and worth saving."

–George Harris as Kingsley Shacklebolt in *Harry Potter and the Deathly Hollows: Part 1* (2010)

"I think the best thing we can do is to let people know that each one of them is precious."

–Tom Hanks as Fred Rogers in *A Beautiful Day in the Neighborhood* (2019)

"I have come to believe that every one of us has a personal calling that's as unique as a fingerprint - and the best way to succeed is to discover what you love and then find a way to offer it to others in the form of service, working hard, and also allowing the energy of the universe to lead you."

–Will Smith as Christopher Gardner in *The Pursuit of Happyness* (2006)

"Every horse is good for something."

–Chris Cooper as Tom Smith in *Seabiscuit* (2003)

"You can't blend in when you were born to stand out."

–Izabela Vidovic as Via in *Wonder* (2017)

"Sometimes it is the people who no one imagines anything of who do the things that no one can imagine."

–Benedict Cumberbatch as Alan Turing in *The Imitation Game* (2014)

You Are of Great Worth

"You are unique; you are irreplaceable," said Elder Holland. "The loss of even one voice diminishes every other singer in this great mortal choir of ours."[5] Each one of us is a distinctive being. "God is your Father. He loves you. He and your Mother in heaven value you beyond any measure," proclaimed Sister Joy D. Jones, Primary General President. "You are unique. One of a kind, made of the eternal intelligence which gives you claim upon eternal life. Let there be no question in your mind about your value as an individual."[6] The movies also talk about our individual value, and the gospel even answers the famous query of Snow White's witch. "In pageants, there is only one declared the fairest of them all," pointed out Elder Lynn G. Robbins of the Seventy. "But with the Lord there is no competition. All have an equal privilege to have His image engraven upon their countenance."[7]

"Magic mirror on the wall, who's the fairest one of all?"

–Lucille La Verne as Evil Queen in *Snow White and the Seven Dwarfs* (1937)

Fiona: "But, I don't understand. I'm supposed to be beautiful."
Shrek: "But you are beautiful."

–Cameron Diaz as Princess Fiona and Mike Myers as Shrek in *Shrek* (2001)

---

[5] Jeffrey R. Holland, "Songs Sung and Unsung," April 2017 General Conference.
[6] Joy D. Jones, "Value Beyond Measure," October 2017 General Conference.
[7] Lynn G. Robbins, "True Beauty," November 2008 General Conference.

"Got to ask yourself this question: 'Am I gonna believe all them bad things them fools say about me today?' You hear me? 'Am I gonna believe all them bad things them fools say about me today?' All right? As for your mama, she didn't pick her life. It picked her. But you, you're gonna do something big with yours. You wait and see."

–Cicely Tyson as Constantine Jefferson in *The Help* (2011)

"I am not a prize to be won!"

–Linda Larkin as Jasmine in *Aladdin* (1992)

"Do you realize how many events, choices, that had to occur since the birth of the universe leading to the making of you, just exactly the way you are?"

–Oprah Winfrey as Mrs. Which in *A Wrinkle in Time* (2018)

"If you know that you came through when people are counting on you, you'll be able to face anything."

–Ed Skrein as Dick Best in *Midway* (2019)

"Hud saw something in you that you don't even see in yourself."

–Chris Cooper as Smokey in *Cars 3* (2017)

"You're not nearly as boring as you pretend to be."

–Eddie Izzard as Garrett in *Every Day* (2018)

"I'm just Ken and I'm enough. And I'm great at doing stuff."

–Ryan Gosling as Ken in *Barbie* (2023)

"You deserve so much more than you think you do."
–Ben Affleck as Ben Holmes in *Forces of Nature* (1999)

"I hope you know that you made today a very special day by just your being you. There's no one in the whole world like you, and I like you just the way you are."
–Tom Hanks as Fred Rogers in *A Beautiful Day in the Neighborhood* (2019)

Believe in Yourself

You may be of great worth, but it is all for naught if you don't believe it and you limit yourself. "Don't limit yourself and don't let others convince you that you are limited in what you can do," President Monson admonished. "You can achieve what you believe you can. Trust and believe and have faith," he said.[8] It helps when so many others believe in you, but ultimately YOU have to believe in YOU. "Good people believe in you. We believe in you, your parents and brothers and sisters believe in you, and God expects the best from you," said Elder David B. Haight of the Twelve. However, he added, "You must believe in yourself."[9] In the movies, similar advice is given by a lion, a boxer, a Lost Boy, and more.

---

[8] Thomas S. Monson, "Living the Abundant Life," *Ensign,* January 2012.
[9] David B. Haight, "A Time for Preparation," November 1991 General Conference.

"Believe in yourself and there will come a day when others will have no choice but to believe with you."

–James Earl Jones as Mufasa in *The Lion King* (2019)

"Nothing is real if you don't believe in who you are!"

–Sylvester Stallone as Rocky Balboa in *Rocky III* (1982)

"The Sphinxes' eyes stay closed, until someone who does not feel his own worth tries to pass by."

–Sydney Bromley as Engywook in *The NeverEnding Story* (1984)

"I believe that if everyone sees what just a few people become when they wholly embrace their gifts, others will awaken. Belief in oneself is contagious. We give each other permission to be superheroes. We will never awaken otherwise."

–Samuel L. Jackson as Elijah Price in *Glass* (2019)

"And the thing is, I really don't care what people think about me... because I believe in myself. And I know that things are gonna be okay."

–Hilary Duff as Sam in *A Cinderella Story* (2004)

"A person should not believe in an '-ism', he should believe in himself. I quote John Lennon, 'I don't believe in Beatles, I just believe in me.' Good point there."

–Matthew Broderick as Ferris Bueller in *Ferris Bueller's Day Off* (1986)

"Do you want to know a secret, Alice? You are as special as you think you are."

–Alyson Court as Princess in *The Care Bears Adventure in Wonderland* (1987)

"Sometimes our strengths lie beneath the surface … far beneath, in some cases."

–Auli'i Cravalho as Moana in *Moana* (2016)

"Don't doubt me, but most importantly don't doubt yourself... you are extraordinary."

–Lewis MacDougal as Nibs in *Pan* (2015)

"You do not yet realize your importance. You have only begun to discover your power."

–James Earl Jones as Darth Vader in *Star Wars: Episode V - The Empire Strikes Back* (1980)

"Show yourself. Step into your power."

–Idina Menzel as Elsa in *Frozen 2* (2019)

"I'm made of wax, Larry. What are you made of?"

–Robin Williams as Teddy Roosevelt in *Night at the Museum* (2006)

"You made the biggest mistake of your life. . . . Underestimating who I am."

–Rosa Salazar as Alita in *Alita: Battle Angel* (2019)

Be True to Who You Are

Be proud of who you are. Be the best you that you can be. Be true to yourself. "How very important it is to be true to ourselves," said President Hinckley. "Be true to yourselves and the best you have within you. That best is very good."[10] This goodness includes your high standards and your Christlike values. "Never be afraid to tell people what you believe in and what your standards are," said Elder Claudio D. Zivic of the Seventy. "You don't need to hide who you are."[11] Not being ashamed of who we are is a theme in many film scripts, as well. We must discover our true identity and hold fast to it. "Be a ray of light," encouraged Elder Holland. "Be your best self and let your character shine."[12]

"Don't ever wish to be anything but what you are."
–Barbara Cook as Mother in *Thumbelina* (1994)

"There's no one I'd rather be, than me!"
–John C. Riley as Ralph in *Wreck it Ralph* (2012)

"I cannot hide who I am."
–Ming-Na Wen as Mulan in *Mulan* (1998)

"Don't be afraid of who you are."
–Daisy Ridley as Rey in *Star Wars: Episode IX – The Rise of Skywalker* (2019)

---

[10] Gordon B. Hinckley, "Stand True and Faithful," April 1996 General Conference.
[11] Claudio D. Zivic, "Strength to Follow the Lord," *Friend*, June 2009.
[12] Quoted in "Elder Holland to BYU Graduates: 'Get Out There and … Be a Ray of Light'," *Church News*, 30 April 2018.

“Jasmine, I do love you, but I’ve got to stop pretending to be something I’m not.”

–Scott Weinger as Aladdin in *Aladdin* (1992)

“Nobody owes nobody nothin'. You owe yourself.”

–Sylvester Stallone as Rocky Balboa in *Rocky III* (1982)

“The measure of a person, of a hero, is how well they succeed at being who they are.”

–Rene Russo as Frigga in *Thor: The Dark World* (2013)

<u>Gael:</u> “When I grow up, I want to be just like you.”
<u>Lucy:</u> “When you grow up, you should be just like you.”

–Arabella Morton as Gael and Georgie Henley as Lucy Pevensie in *The Chronicles of Narnia: The Voyage of the Dawn Treader* (2010)

“You cannot live your life to please others. The choice must be yours.”

–Anne Hathaway as White Queen in *Alice and Wonderland* (2010)

“There's a lot of people saying a lot of things, but in the end you gotta listen to yourself.”

–Austin Butler as Elvis Presley in *Elvis* (2022)

"From the very beginning I've always made a statement. Not everyone appreciated that. But I wasn't for everyone."

–Emma Stone as Estella in *Cruella* (2021)

"Trust yourself. Think for yourself. Act for yourself. Speak for yourself. Be yourself. Imitation is suicide."

–Robin Williams as John Keating in *Dead Poets Society* (1989)

"The moment you become embarrassed of who you are, you lose yourself."

–Elliott Gould as Reuben Tishkoff in *Ocean's Thirteen* (2007)

"Your identity is your most valuable possession. Protect it."

–Holly Hunter as Elastigirl in *The Incredibles* (2004)

"Self-respect permeates every aspect of your existence. If you don't have respect for yourself, you're not gonna get it from anyone else."

–Morgan Freeman as Principal Joe Clark in *Lean on Me* (1989)

"Cletus, we are supposed to be who we are and I'm just fine with who I am!"

–Eddie Murphy as Mama Klump in *Nutty Professor II: The Klumps* (2000)

Inside Us is What Counts

The Bible reminds us, "the Lord seeth not as man seeth; for man looketh on the outward appearance, but the Lord looketh on the heart."[13] Likewise, latter-day leaders and many movies tell us that it is the inside of us that counts. "The gospel teaches us that true beauty is more than skin-deep," reminded Elder Robbins.[14] We not only have the potential to be beautiful on the inside, but we have a great inner strength there we can tap into, as well. "You have an inexhaustible, divine source of strength burning inside of you," said Elder Gary E. Stevenson of the Twelve.[15]

"It's hard for many people to believe that there are extraordinary things inside themselves, as well as others. I hope you can keep an open mind."

–Samuel L. Jackson as Elijah Price in *Unbreakable* (2000)

"I have my own soul! My own spark of divine fire!"

–Rex Harrison as Professor Henry Higgins in *My Fair Lady* (1964)

"In the heart of a Jedi lies her strength."

–Freddie Prinze Jr. as Kanan Jarrus in *Star Wars: Episode IX - The Rise of Skywalker* (2019)

---

[13] 1 Samuel 16:7

[14] Lynn G. Robbins, "True Beauty," *New Era*, November 2008.

[15] Gary E. Stevenson, "5 Ways to Conquer Fear," *New Era*, February 2017.

"In my old life, I longed for someone to see what was special in me. You did, and for that, you'll always be in my heart. But what I really needed was for me to see it. And now I do."

–Halle Berry as Catwoman in *Catwoman* (2004)

"She warned him not to be deceived by appearances, for beauty is found within."

–David Ogden Stiers as Narrator in *Beauty and the Beast* (1991)

"I made you look like a prince on the outside. But I didn't change anything on the inside."

–Will Smith as Genie in *Aladdin* (2019)

"If come from inside you, always right one."

–Pat Morita as Mr. Miyagi in *The Karate Kid* (1984)

"Everyone runs in her own way, or his own way. And where does the power come from, to see the race to its end? From within."

–Ian Charleson as Eric Liddell in *Chariots of Fire* (1981)

13

TRUTH, HONESTY & INTEGRITY

It is the pinnacle of our Articles of Faith that "We believe in being honest, true, chaste, benevolent, virtuous, and in doing good to all men." We must seek the truth and tell the truth; for truth is absolute, even if not always easy. We learn from many films and scripture alike that honesty always wins in the end, and that real heroes are characters of integrity and goodness.

Seek the Truth, Tell the Truth

As Latter-day Saints, we have a solemn duty to both seek for truth, and to speak truthfully. "The pursuit, discovery, and application of truth are what we are on this earth to discover," said President Uchtdorf.[1] The boy Joseph Smith sought wisdom and to know the truth of which church to join, for example. We, too, can seek divine truths. "The greatest quest is a search for God—to determine his reality," said President Hunter.[2] In all of our dealings, we can also be honest and tell the truth. "May we be people of honesty and integrity, trying to do the right thing at all times and in all circumstances," pleaded President Monson.[3]

"Our goal is one and the same: the pursuit of Truth."
–Matthew McConaughey as Palmer Joss in *Contact* (1997)

---

[1] Quoted in "Truth Is Complete and Universal, President Uchtdorf Says," *Church News*, 10 March 2014.
[2] Howard W. Hunter "To Know God," October 1974 General Conference.
[3] Thomas S. Monson, "Until We Meet Again," October 2014 General Conference.

Mary Lou: "Are you a seeker? A seeker after truth?"
Newt: "I'm more of a chaser, really."

–Samantha Morton as Mary Lou, Eddie Redmayne as Newt in *Fantastic Beasts and Where to Find Them* (2016)

"Not all who wander are aimless. Especially not those who seek truth beyond tradition; beyond definition; beyond the image."

–Kirsten Dunst as Betty Warren in *Mona Lisa Smile* (2003)

"Listen to your heart, and you'll find the truth!"

–Billie Mae Richards as Tender Heart Bear in *The Care Bears Movie* (1985)

"Search your feelings, you *know* it to be true!"

–James Earl Jones as Darth Vader in *Star Wars: Episode V - The Empire Strikes Back* (1980)

"If he was absolutely determined to discover the truth, there's no way we could prevent him."

–Ed Harris as Christof in *The Truman Show* (1998)

"A hero always tells the truth no matter what people think about him or no matter what the consequences are."

–Thomas Haden Church as Ray Wincott in *Max* (2015)

"You want a good life? It's not complicated. Tell the girl you love that you love her. And tell the truth to everyone whenever you can."

–Robert Carlyle as John Lennon in *Yesterday* (2019)

"You see, Pinocchio, a lie keeps growing and growing until it's as plain as the nose on your face."

–Evelyn Venable as The Blue Fairy in *Pinocchio* (1940)

"The rule here is: always tell the truth."

–Julia Sawalha as Ginger in *Chicken Run* (2000)

"Tell them the truth unvarnished."

–Ben Mendelsohn as King George VI in *Darkest Hour* (2017)

Truth is Absolute

A number of films agree with church leaders that Truth–with a capital "T"–is real. "Absolute truth exists in a world that increasingly disdains and dismisses absolutes," taught Elder Bednar.[4] Earth really is round (not flat), more lions are eaten by gazelles each year than gazelles eaten by lions, and gravity will act upon us regardless of any parliamentary proclamation. "The thing about truth is that it exists beyond belief. It is true even if nobody believes it," said President Uchtdorf.[5]

---

[4] David A. Bednar, "Come and See," October 2014 General Conference.
[5] Dieter F. Uchtdorf, "What Is Truth?" *BYU Speeches*, 13 January 2013.

These include gospel truths about our Heavenly Parents and our origin and potential as their children, the reality of Jesus Christ acting as a mediator to help us return to our Heavenly Home, and the restoration of the priesthood keys in modern times that authorize sacred covenants that bind us to loved ones beyond this world. "I am the way, the truth, and the life," said Jesus, "and the truth shall make you free."[6] A knowledge of Him is of the most precious truths. "Oh say, what is truth?" asks the hymn penned by John Jaques, who then answers, "'Tis the fairest gem that the riches of worlds can produce."[7]

"Some things are true whether you believe them or not."
–Nicholas Cage as Seth in *City of Angels* (1998)

"Some things are absolutely true."
–Joel Courtney as Greg Laurie in *Jesus Revolution* (2023)

"All of it. It's all true."
–Harrison Ford as Han Solo in *Star Wars: Episode VII—The Force Awakens* (2015)

"You can only have the truth. And the truth is enough. The truth is beautiful. . . The truth is bigger than all of us."
–Gal Gadot as Diana Prince in *Wonder Woman 1984* (2020)

---

[6] John 14:6 and John 8:32
[7] Hymn 272, "Oh Say, What Is Truth?"

"If you are a minority of one, the truth is the truth."

–Ben Kingsley as Mahatma Gandhi in *Gandhi* (1982)

"Just because you refuse to believe something doesn't make it true. Or false."

–Kate Hudson as Tess Finnegan in *Fool's Gold* (2008)

"The truth sounds insane sometimes, but that doesn't mean it's not."

–Lou Romano as Linguini in *Ratatouille* (2007)

"Some things are always true. Some things never change."

–Kristen Bell as Anna in *Frozen 2* (2019)

"Just because you can't understand something doesn't mean it's wrong."

–Rickie Sorensen as Arthur in *The Sword and the Stone* (1963)

"The truth is always quiet; the lies are always loud. The truth is simple."

–Julia Campbell as Kay Smith in in *Jesus Revolution* (2023)

Truth is Not Always Easy

It is trickier than ever to discern fact and fiction. "Never in the history of the world have we had easier access to more information—some of it true, some of it false, and much of it partially true. Consequently, never in the history of the world has it been more important to learn how to correctly discern between truth and error," said President Uchtdorf. "So often the 'truths' we tell ourselves are merely fragments of the truth, and sometimes they're not really the truth at all," he said.[8]

There are half-truths and relative truths out there. Often, even the full truth hurts and is far less convenient to share than a small fib would be. "The guilty taketh the truth to be hard, for it cutteth them to the very center," wrote the Prophet Nephi.[9] Some of our favorite films explore this truth that dealing with the truth is not always easy!

"Oh no! These facts and opinions look so similar!"
–Amy Poehler as Joy in *Inside Out* (2015)

"The truth rarely makes sense when you omit key details."
–Florence Pugh as Yelena Belova in *Black Widow* (2021)

"It's harder to take things on trust from people speaking half-truths."
–John David Washington as Protagonist in *Tenet* (2020)

"Sometimes the truth does taste like a mouthful of worms."
–Martin Landau as Leonard in *North by Northwest* (1959)

---

8 Dieter F. Uchtdorf, "What Is Truth?" *BYU Speeches*, 13 January 2013.
9 1 Nephi 16:2

"The truth is a matter of circumstances, it's not all things to all people at the same time."

–Chris Evans as Steve Rogers in *Captain America: Winter Soldier* (2014)

"Many of the truths that we cling to depend on our point of view."

–Alec Guinness as Obi-Wan Kenobi in *Star Wars: Episode VI - Return of the Jedi* (1983)

"The truth doesn't always win friends, but it certainly influences people."

–Robin Williams as Batty Koda in *FernGully: The Last Rainforest* (1992)

"Pay no attention to that man behind the curtain."

–Frank Morgan as The Wizard of Oz in *The Wizard of Oz* (1939)

"The complexity and the gray lie not in the truth but what you do with the truth once you have it."

–Daniel Craig as Benoit Blanc in *Knives Out* (2019)

"The truth. It is a beautiful and terrible thing, and should therefore be treated with great caution."

–Richard Harris as Albus Dumbledore in *Harry Potter and the Sorcerer's Stone* (2001)

"You sit on a throne of lies."

–Will Ferrell as Buddy the Elf in *Elf* (2003)

"Sometimes the truth is painful, Frank. But it's made your cheeks rosy and your eyes bright!"

–Carol Kane as Ghost of Christmas Present in *Scrooged* (1988)

Honesty Always Wins in the End

"Thou shalt not steal," declared Jehovah from Sinai. "Thou shalt not bear false witness against thy neighbour."[10] We are commanded to be honest. We are blessed in the end with the clear conscious and good night sleep that comes to those with integrity. And we know that a tangled web of dishonesty will be a snare in the end. "Each lie, each deception, each act of dishonesty combines to create a monster that can destroy your character and your life," warned President Hunter.[11] There are (sadly) plenty of movie quotes about the ends justifying the means and celebrating dishonesty. But fortunately, hidden in Hollywood, we find some great gems that jibe with gospel teachings.

"You can never go wrong with the truth."

–Brenda Blethyn as Polly Cassotto in *Beyond the Sea* (2004)

"Never put passion in front of principle. Even if you win, you lose."

–Pat Morita as Mr. Miyagi in *The Karate Kid* (1984)

---

[10] Exodus 20:15-16

[11] Howard W. Hunter, "Be Honest with Yourself," *New Era*, February 1978.

"Truth, like oil, will in time rise to surface."

–Sidney Toler as Charlie Chan in *Charlie Chan's Murder Cruise* (1940)

"Women always figure out the truth. Always."

–Harrison Ford as Han Solo in *Star Wars: Episode VII—The Force Awakens* (2015)

"One honest voice can carry over a crowd."

–Reese Witherspoon as Elle Woods in *Legally Blonde 2: Red, White & Blonde* (2003)

"If you want to get someone's trust you have to give a little trust first."

–Awkwafina as Sisu in *Raya and the Last Dragon* (2021)

"A faithful heart makes wishes come true."

–Chang Chen as Lo 'Dark Cloud' in *Crouching Tiger, Hidden Dragon* (2000)

Integrity and Goodness of Character

The best heroes in the movies are those of goodness and integrity. "Men who have 'integrity of heart' are men to be trusted—because trust is built on integrity," said Elder Richard J. Maynes of the Seventy. "Being a man of integrity simply means your intentions, as well as your actions, are pure and righteous in all aspects of your life, both in public and in private," he said.[12] Living lives of character and light will bring honor to your name and to your family. And as the Bible teaches, "A good name is rather to be chosen than great riches, and loving favour rather than silver and gold."[13]

"A ninja is honest and good. His mind, body and spirit are one. He has self-control. He has discipline."

–Michael Treanor as Rocky in *3 Ninjas* (1992)

"I know you are a man of conviction, a person who knows the difference between what is wrong and what is right."

–Tom Hanks as Fred Rogers in *A Beautiful Day in the Neighborhood* (2019)

"There's no place out there for graft, or greed, or lies, or compromise with human liberties."

–Jimmy Stewart as Jefferson Smith in *Mr. Smith Goes to Washington* (1939)

"Wrong is wrong, even when it helps you."

–Robin Williams as Popeye in *Popeye* (1980)

"Do you trust me?"

–Scott Weinger as Aladdin in *Aladdin* (1992)

---

[12] Richard J. Maynes, "Earning the Trust of the Lord and Your Family," October 2017 General Conference.

[13] Proverbs 22:1

"You are a good man, with a good heart. And it's hard for a good man to be a king."

–John Kani as T'Chaka in *Black Panther* (2018)

"I would rather be a good man than a great king."

–Chis Hemsworth as Thor in *Thor: The Dark World* (2013)

"Well, anything worth doing is worth doing right."

–Tom Hanks as Jimmy Dugan in *A League of Their Own* (1992)

"We are men of action. Lies do not become us."

–Cary Elwes as Westley in *The Princess Bride* (1987)

"I promise. And when I promise something, I never, ever break that promise."

–Mandy Moore as Rapunzel in *Tangled* (2010)

"Gentlemen do not steal ladies' crowns!"

–Jennifer Saunders as Queen Elizabeth in *Minions* (2015)

"I believe there's a hero in all of us, that keeps us honest, gives us strength, makes us noble."

–Rosemary Harris as Aunt May in *Spider-Man 2* (2004)

"I'm here to fight for truth, and justice, and the American way."

–Christopher Reeve as Superman in *Superman* (1978)

"I may not know much of law Mr. Felder, but I know what's right and what's wrong. And I know what you're asking is wrong."

–Henry Fonda as Abraham Lincoln in *Young Mr. Lincoln* (1939)

"Arm thyself with this enchanted Shield of Virtue, and this mighty Sword of Truth, for these weapons of righteousness will triumph over evil."

–Verna Felton as Flora in *Sleeping Beauty* (1959)

"She has brought honor to her ancestors, to her family, to her village, and to her country."

–Donnie Yen as Commander Tung in *Mulan* (2020)

14

KNOWLEDGE, WISDOM, & JUDGMENT

Some of our favorite films dovetail with gospel teachings about learning and education, gaining knowledge, learning life lessons, increasing our intelligence and perspective, and making wise judgments (while preparing for our own Final Judgment). What can we learn from both divine sources and Hollywood about learning?

Learning and Education

Getting a good education–both religious and secular–has been an important tenet of the faith since the days of Joseph Smith and his School of the Prophets. "Seek ye out of the best books words of wisdom; seek learning, even by study and also by faith," proclaims the Doctrine and Covenants.[1] With the world increasingly complex and competitive, the need for education is greater than ever. "You must get all of the education that you possibly can," said President Hinckley. "You will be expected to put forth great effort and to use your best talents to make your way to the most wonderful future of which you are capable."[2]

There are great films about educational triumph, and prophets continue to encourage us to keep learning, as well. "Continue your education, wherever you are, whatever your interest and opportunity may be," taught President Nelson. "Determine how you can best serve your family and society and prepare well."[3]

---

[1] D&C 88:118

[2] Gordon B. Hinckley, "Stay on the High Road," April 2004 General Conference.

[3] Russell M. Nelson, "Where is Wisdom?" October 1992 General Conference.

"There's only one thing to do: Learn all we can."

–Octavia Spencer as Dorothy in *Hidden Figures* (2016)

"You can't grow up without a decent education, you know."

–Karl Swenson as Merlin in *The Sword in the Stone* (1963)

"When in doubt, go to the library."

–Rupert Grint as Ron Weasley in *Harry Potter and the Chamber of Secrets* (2002)

"Either of you guys ever go to Sunday school?"

–Harrison Ford as Indiana Jones in *Raiders of the Lost Ark* (1981)

"The Good Book did not arrive by facsimile from heaven."

–Ian McKellen as Sir Leigh Teabing in *The Da Vinci Code* (2006)

"We have tried to teach other Sky People. It is hard to fill a cup which is already full."

–C. C. H. Pounder as Mo'at in *Avatar* (2009)

"Write. In my religion, we're taught that every living thing, every leaf, every bird, is only alive because it contains the secret word for life. That's the only difference between us and a lump of clay. A word. Words are life."

–Ben Schnetzer as Max Vandenburg in *The Book Thief* (2013)

"Read the directions and directly you will be directed in the right direction."

–Joseph Kearns as Doorknob in *Alice in Wonderland* (1951)

"I went to kindergarten, I know how the alphabet works."

–Steve Carell as Gru in *Despicable Me* (2010)

"Students will rise to the level of expectation, Señor Molina."

–Edward James Olmos as Jaime Escalante in *Stand and Deliver* (1988)

"A teacher has two jobs: fill young minds with knowledge, yes, but more important, give those minds a compass so that that knowledge doesn't go to waste."

–Olympia Dukakis as Principal Helen Jacobs in *Mr. Holland's Opus* (1995)

Knowledge

Learning and education can lead to knowledge, which is a divine value. "Whatever principle of intelligence we attain unto in this life, it will rise with us in the resurrection," reads a well-known verse in the Doctrine and Covenants. "And if a person gains more knowledge and intelligence in this life through his diligence and obedience than another, he will have so much the advantage in the world to come."[4] This eternal principle has been part of the gospel from the beginning. "What are we here for?" asked Brigham Young. "To learn to enjoy more, and to

[4] D&C 130:18-19

increase in knowledge and in experience," he said.[5] As the movies sometimes show, the treasure of knowledge can be a light in our lives.

"In a dark place we find ourselves, and a little more knowledge lights our way."

–Frank Oz as Yoda in *Star Wars: Episode III – Revenge of the Sith* (2005)

"Obedience without understanding is a blindness."

–Anne Bancroft as Annie Sullivan in *The Miracle Worker* (1962)

"The Ugha word for gold translates as 'treasure'. But their treasure wasn't gold. It was knowledge. Knowledge was their treasure."

–Harrison Ford as Indiana Jones in *Indiana Jones and the Kingdom of the Crystal Skull* (2008)

"Not all treasure's silver and gold, mate."

–Johnny Depp as Jack Sparrow in *Pirates of the Caribbean: The Curse of the Black Pearl* (2003)

"Knowing is good, but knowing everything is better."

–Tom Hanks as Bailey in *The Circle* (2017)

---

[5] *Discourses of Brigham Young*, Selected by John A. Widtsoe, 1941, p. 87.

"There might be a lot we don't know about each other. You know, people seldom go to the trouble of scratching the surface of things to find the inner truth."

–Jimmy Stewart as Alfred Kralik in *The Shop Around the Corner* (1940)

"Sometimes it's not enough to know the meaning of things, sometimes we have to know what things don't mean as well."

–Bob Dylan as Jack Fate in *Masked and Anonymous* (2003)

"It's not a bad thing finding out that you don't have all the answers. You start asking the right questions. . . Anyone who's ever going to find his way in this world, has to start by admitting he doesn't know."

–Stellan Skarsgård as Erik Selvig in *Thor* (2011)

"Fifteen hundred years ago, everybody knew that the Earth was the center of the universe. Five hundred years ago, everybody knew that the Earth was flat. And fifteen minutes ago, you knew that humans were alone on this planet. Imagine what you'll know tomorrow."

–Tommy Lee Jones as Kay in *Men in Black* (1997)

"Well, you must realize, Harriet, knowing everything won't do you a bit of good unless you use it to put beauty in this world."

–Rosie O'Donnell as Ole Golly in *Harriet the Spy* (1996)

"Isn't it nice to know a lot... and a little bit not..."

–Lilla Crawford as Little Red Riding Hood in *Into the Woods* (2014)

Life Lessons

We can learn great knowledge beyond the classroom. In fact, our street smarts never are learned in the library. "You have an individual responsibility to seek learning," taught Sister Mary N. Cook of the Young Women General Presidency. "Some of your most important learning will be outside of the classroom," she said.[6] In all ways we learn best "line upon line, precept upon precept."[7] In the world, we can learn from our mistakes and become better than we were. "Learning the lessons of the past allows you to walk boldly in the light without running the risk of stumbling in the darkness," pointed out President Ballard.[8]

"The world is not in your books and maps. It is out there."

–Ian McKellen as Gandalf in *The Hobbit: An Unexpected Journey* (2012)

"This is what happens when you leave home. You meet... people."

–Steve Coogan as Phileas Fogg in *Around the World in 80 Days* (2004)

---

[6] Mary N. Cook, "Seek Learning: You Have a Work to Do," April 2012 General Conference.

[7] Isaiah 28:10

[8] M. Russell Ballard, "Learning the Lessons of the Past," April 2009 General Conference.

"If you only do what you can do, you will never be more than who you are."

–Dustin Hoffman as Shifu in *Kung Fu Panda 3* (2016)

"First learn stand, then learn fly. Nature rule, Daniel-san, not mine."

–Pat Morita as Mr. Miyagi in *The Karate Kid* (1984)

"One step at a time. One punch at a time. One round at a time."

–Sylvester Stallone as Rocky Balboa in *Creed* (2015)

"The past can hurt. But from the way I see it, you can either run from it or learn from it."

–Robert Guillaume as Rafiki in *The Lion King* (1994)

"Some days, my childhood feels so very far away. And others, I can almost see it. The magical land of my youth, like a beautiful dream of when the whole world felt like a promise and the lessons that lay ahead yet unseen. Looking back, I wish I'd listened, wish I'd watched more closely and understood. But sometimes you can't see what you're learning until you come out the other side."

–Gal Gadot as Diana Prince in *Wonder Woman 1984* (2020)

Intelligence and Perspective

"The glory of God is intelligence, or, in other words, light and truth," proclaimed the Lord to Joseph Smith.[9] Part of growing our intelligence is learning new perspectives. "As you live righteously, you will find that during your lifetime your perspective will enlarge many, many times," said President Ballard.[10] Jedis, wizards, and scientists have fun thoughts on intelligence and perspective, too.

"The ability to speak does not make you intelligent."
–Liam Neeson as Qui-Gon Jinn in *Star Wars: Episode I - The Phantom Menace* (1999)

"And there seems to be no sign of intelligent life anywhere."
–Tim Allen as Buzz Lightyear in *Toy Story* (1995)

"There's no such thing as the unknown, only things temporarily hidden, temporarily not understood."
–Chris Pine as Captain James T. Kirk in *Star Trek Beyond* (2016)

"When you get a different vantage point, it changes your perspective ... It allows us to see things that maybe we should have seen a long time ago."
–Ryan Gosling as Neil Armstrong in *First Man* (2018)

---

9 D&C 93:36
10 Neil L. Andersen, "Seeing Through the Generations," *BYU Speeches*, 16 May 2006.

"When you change the view from where you stood, the things you view will change for good."

–Emily Blunt as Mary Poppins in *Mary Poppins Returns* (2018)

"Monster is a relative term. To a canary, a cat is a monster. We're just used to being the cat."

–Henry Wu as B.D. Wong in *Jurassic World* (2015)

"There's always a bigger fish."

–Liam Neeson as Qui-Gon Jinn in *Star Wars: Episode I - The Phantom Menace* (1999)

"The mind is a complex and many-layered thing."

–Alan Rickman as Severus Snape in *Harry Potter and the Order of the Phoenix* (2007)

"You're not thinking fourth dimensionally!"

–Christopher Lloyd as Dr. Emmett Brown in *Back to the Future Part III* (1990)

Judgment

As we gain knowledge, we will hopefully use wisdom in making good judgments. The movies have ideas about exercising common sense, not judging others superficially, and making good calls. Yoda, for instance, would like the Biblical advice to "Look not on his countenance, or on the height of his stature; because I have refused him: for the Lord seeth not as man seeth; for man looketh on the outward appearance, but the Lord looketh on the heart."[11] But in the end we are also all judged by our Maker, and films say a bit about that, as well. President Monson also spoke of that time. "There is a time of reckoning—even a balancing of the ledger. It's called Judgment Day, even the Big Exam of Life. Are we prepared?"[12]

"You can't kneel in the middle of a highway and live to tell the tale."

–Morgan Freeman as God in *Bruce Almighty* (2003)

"Sometimes a person we love, through no fault of their own, can't see past the end of his nose."

–Julie Andrews as Mary Poppins in *Mary Poppins* (1964)

"For a true hero isn't measured by the size of his strength, but by the strength of his heart."

–Rip Torn as Zeus in *Hercules* (1997)

Tibby: "You were right, and I was wrong, but I'm wrong about most people."
Bailey: "The important thing is you always change your mind about them."

–Amber Tamblyn as Tibby and Jenna Boyd as Bailey in *The Sisterhood of the Traveling Pants* (2005)

---

[11] 1 Samuel 16:7

[12] Thomas S. Monson, "Standards of Strength," *New Era*, October 2008.

“Don't you judge people by their appearance.”

–Gene Wilder as Avram in *The Frisco Kid* (1979)

“Judge me by my size, do you?”

–Frank Oz as Yoda in *Star Wars: Episode V - The Empire Strikes Back* (1980)

“This is the place.”

–Dean Jagger as Brigham Young in *Brigham Young* (1940)

“But all accounts are balanced in the end.”

–Ben Affleck as Bruce Wayne in *Batman vs Superman* (2016)

“I would rather stand with God and be judged by the world, than stand with the world and be judged by God.”

–Melissa Joan Hart as Grace Wesley in *God's Not Dead 2* (2016)

15

OVERCOMING EVIL & ADVERSITY

Perhaps one of the greatest gifts of inspiring wisdom from both religious and secular sources is a blueprint of how to get through life's challenges. From both we learn that everyone has challenges and that we all suffer from pain, worry, and disappointment. We learn that temptation is real, that bad guys do harm, and that fear leads to anger and anger leads to hate. But most importantly, movies and the gospel alike can teach us how to overcome adversity and bend trials to our advantage!

Everyone Has Challenges

Elder Anthony D. Perkins of the Seventy once pointed out this truth: "Regardless of where you live, physical or emotional suffering from a variety of trials and mortal weaknesses has been, is now, or will someday be part of your life."[1] The stories told on the silver screen, of course, require conflict to advance the plot. So, all of Hollywood's protagonists have challenges. But this aspect of film fantasy is actually accurate. "Life is filled with harsh realities that tug at the heart and tear away at the soul," President Ballard declared."[2] These trials are part of the test of life.

"We ALL have to climb mountains, you know. Mountains that go way up high, and mountains that go deep and low."

–Will Smith as Chris Gardner in *The Pursuit of Happyness* (2006)

---

[1] Anthony D. Perkins, "Remember Thy Suffering Saints, O Our God," October 2021 General Conference.

[2] M. Russell Ballard, "Answers to Life's Questions," April 1995 General Conference.

"There is no normal life that is free from pain."

–Tom Hanks as Fred Rogers in *A Beautiful Day in the Neighborhood* (2019)

"Oh, bah! Everybody's got problems. The world's full of problems."

–Karl Swenson as Merlin in *The Sword in the Stone* (1963)

"The world ain't all sunshine and rainbows. It's a very mean and nasty place and I don't care how tough you are, it will beat you to your knees and keep you there permanently if you let it."

–Sylvester Stallone as Rocky Balboa in *Rocky Balboa* (2006)

"We all have marks on our face. This is the map that shows where we've been and it's never, ever ugly."

–Julia Roberts as Isabel in *Wonder* (2017)

"I don't know why terrible things happen to us sometimes. But I have to believe that something good is going to come out of this."

–Carrie Underwood as Sarah Hill in *Soul Surfer* (2011)

"We seem to be made to suffer. It's our lot in life."

–Anthony Daniels as C3PO in *Star Wars: Episode IV - A New Hope* (1977)

"My life hasn't been what you think it has. We all have our struggles."

–Gal Gadot as Diana Prince in *Wonder Woman 1984* (2020)

"Grief is never an easy burden to bear."

–Marek Wiedman as Funeral Minister in *The Sisterhood of the Traveling Pants* (2005)

Pain, Worry, and Disappointment

Not only do we all face challenges, but none of us are free from pain. "In this mortal life, each of us is going to experience pain in one form or another," taught Elder Hales. "As we put our faith and trust in the Lord, we must battle our pain day by day and sometimes hour by hour, even moment by moment."[3] Movies provide powerful insights about the pains of this world, and so do other general authorities. "No pain that we suffer, no trial that we experience is wasted," declared Elder Paul V. Johnson of the Seventy. "All that we suffer and all that we endure, especially when we endure it patiently, builds up our characters, purifies our hearts, expands our souls, and makes us more tender and charitable," he continued. "It is through sorrow and suffering, toil and tribulation, that we gain the education that we come here to acquire."[4]

---

[3] Robert D. Hales, "Healing Soul and Body," October 1998 General Conference.

[4] Paul V. Johnson, "More Than Conquerors through Him That Loved Us," April 2011 General Conference.

Disappointment and worry cause their own pain, often needlessly. "Don't worry about those things which you cannot change. If something can be done, do it. If nothing can be done, don't worry about it," said Elder George I. Cannon of the Seventy.[5] This reminds me of Reinhold Niebuhr's Serenity Prayer, quoted in the movie *Home Run*, listed below.

"Life is pain, highness. Anyone who says differently is selling something."

–Cary Elwes as Westley in *The Princess Bride* (1987)

"Pain is God's megaphone to rouse a deaf world."

–Anthony Hopkins as C.S. Lewis in *Shadowlands* (1993)

"That's the thing about pain, it demands to be felt."

–Ansel Elgort as Augustus Waters in *The Fault in Our Stars* (2014)

"Uh, no pain, no gain?"

–Christopher Reeve as Clark Kent in *Superman IV* (1987)

"Stop running from it. Let that pain become your inspiration."

–Trace Adkins as Brickell in *I Can Only Imagine* (2018)

---

5 George I. Cannon, "Today-A Day of Eternity," October 1991 General Conference.

"Without suffering, there'd be no compassion. I hope you feel things you never felt before. I hope you meet people with a different point of view."

–Mandy Moore as Jamie Sullivan in *A Walk to Remember* (2002)

"If you expect disappointment, then you can never really get disappointed."

–Zendaya as MJ in *Spider Man: No Way Home* (2021)

"Mirabel and I were having a conversation about how I carry too much, so I tried not to carry so much, but I realized it was putting me behind, and I knew I was letting everyone down."

–Jess Darrow as Luisa Madrigal in *Encanto* (2021)

"My philosophy is that worrying means you suffer twice."

–Eddie Redmayne as Newt Scamander in *Fantastic Beasts and Where to Find Them* (2016)

"God grant me the serenity to accept the things I cannot change, courage to change the things I can, and the wisdom to know the difference."

–Scott Elrod as Cory Brand in *Home Run* (2013)

Temptation

Just as we all face challenges and pain, we also all are tempted to go astray from the paths we should be on. Even the perfect Son of God was tempted while in the flesh and warned us about being led amiss. "Ye must watch and pray always lest ye enter into temptation," He taught, "for Satan desireth to have you, that he may sift you as wheat."[6] Sister Sharon G. Larsen of the Young Women General Presidency was as wise as a wizard when she cautioned us, "Do not encourage a curiosity that ought to be stopped. Pay attention to what you are feeling so you will know when you are feeling unsure or uneasy."[7] President Kimball was likewise as wise as a Jedi Master when he warned, "Our expressions, our voice tones, our movements, our thoughts betray us."[8]

"Be mindful of your thoughts Anakin. They'll betray you."

–Ewan McGregor as Obi-Wan Kenobi in *Star Wars: Episode II - Attack of the Clones* (2002)

"Curiosity is not a sin.... But we should exercise caution with our curiosity... yes, indeed."

–Michael Gambon as Albus Dumbledore in *Harry Potter and the Goblet of Fire* (2005)

---

[6] 3 Nephi 18:18

[7] Sharon G. Larsen, "Standing in Holy Places," April 2002 General Conference.

[8] Spencer W. Kimball, *Conference Report*, April 1954, 106.

"Marty, you can't go losing your judgment every time someone calls you a name. That's exactly what causes you to get into that accident in the future."

–Christopher Lloyd as Dr. Emmett Brown in *Back to the Future, Part III* (1990)

"Being brave doesn't mean you go looking for trouble."

–James Earl Jones as Mufasa in *The Lion King* (1994)

"Satan wears many guises. At times, he is the singer of a lurid song you hear on the radio. At times, the author of a salacious novel."

–Hugh O'Conor as Father Henri in *Chocolat* (2000)

"I've got gadgets and gizmos a-plenty, I've got who's its and what's its galore. You want thingamabobs? I've got twenty. But who cares? No big deal, I want more."

–Jodi Benson as Ariel in *The Little Mermaid* (1989)

"Wine is where the devil finds his darlings."

–Penélope Cruz as Pilar Estravados in *Murder on the Orient Express* (2017)

"When you think you're safe is precisely when you're most vulnerable."

–Takashi Shimura as Kambei Shimada in *Seven Samurai* (1954)

"It's a trap!"

–Tim Rose as Admiral Ackbar in *Star Wars: Episode VI - Return of the Jedi* (1983)

"Stay focused on light when darkness is present."

–Oprah Winfrey as Mrs. Which in *A Wrinkle in Time* (2018)

"Once you start down the dark path, forever will it dominate your destiny."

–Frank Oz as Yoda in *Star Wars: Episode V - The Empire Strikes Back* (1980)

Bad Guys

Most movies have both good guys and bad guys. In life, those who would tempt us to do bad things are usually not Hollywood's space aliens or Nazis, but can even be our friends. "Have confidence to do right and overcome strong negative peer pressure and bad influences," said Elder Scott. "You don't need to compromise your standards to be accepted by good friends."[9]

Yet, movies and church teachings alike acknowledge that the Devil is also very real, as are those who follow his evil ways. "Satan is the greatest imitator, the master deceiver, the arch counterfeiter, and the greatest forger ever in the history of the world," warned President James E. Faust. "He comes into our

[9] Richard G. Scott, "Making the Right Choices," October 1994 General Conference.

lives as a thief in the night. His disguise is so perfect that it is hard to recognize him or his methods. He is a wolf in sheep's clothing."[10] As the Adversary ratchets up his destroying ways in the latter-days, Elder Bruce C. Hafen of the Seventy pointed out his similarities to one of Hollywood's greatest villains. "The Prince of Darkness has dragged out the heavy artillery. He is no longer limited to arrows and swords and BB guns. Now he is Darth Vader, with laser guns, light speeds, and the death star."[11]

"The Devil is that element in human nature that impels us to destroy and debase."

–Marlon Brando as Dr. Moreau in *The Island of Dr. Moreau* (1996)

"Nobody's ever seen the Devil, but we know he exists, don't we?"

–Mai Elizabeth Zetterling as Helga in *The Witches* (2020)

"He's more machine now than man. Twisted and evil."

–Alec Guinness as Obi-Wan Kenobi in *Star Wars: Episode VI - Return of the Jedi* (1983)

"In the beginning, it is always dark."

–Tami Stronach as The Childlike Empress in *The NeverEnding Story* (1984)

---

[10] James E. Faust, "The Devil's Throat," April 2003 General Conference.
[11] Bruce C. Hafen, "The Gospel and Romantic Love," *Ensign*, October 1982.

"It takes a great deal of bravery to stand up to our enemies, but just as much to stand up to our friends."

–Richard Harris as Albus Dumbledore in *Harry Potter and the Sorcerer's Stone* (2001)

"Consider who we're dealing with here. Give a wolf a taste of your leg and he'll ask for your hand."

–Kamatari Fujiwara as Farmer Manzô in *Seven Samurai* (1954)

"Sometimes the devil allows people to live a life free of trouble because he doesn't want them turning to God. Their sin is like a jail cell, except it is all nice and comfy and there doesn't seem to be any reason to leave. The door's wide open. Till one day, time runs out, and the cell door slams shut, and suddenly it's too late."

–Lenore Banks as Mina's Mother in *God's Not Dead* (2014)

"The only devils in the world are those running around in our own hearts. And that is where all our battles ought to be fought."

–Ben Kingsley as Mahatma Gandhi in *Gandhi* (1982)

Fear, Anger, and Hate

Since both movies and Sunday School acknowledge that the Devil is real, let's look at three of his most useful tools: fear, anger, and hate. President Oaks declared, "The devil is the father of contention, and it is he who tempts men to contend with anger. He promotes enmity and hateful relationships among individuals and within groups."[12] As many film stars point out below, fear can hold us back, or worse, slide us into anger and hate. "Let us recognize that fear comes not of God, but rather that this gnawing, destructive element comes from the adversary of truth and righteousness," said President Hinckley. "Fear is the antithesis of faith. It is corrosive in its effects, even deadly."[13] The Apostle Paul was right. "God hath not given us the spirit of fear; but of power, and of love, and of a sound mind," he wrote.[14]

"Fear leads to anger, anger leads to hate, hate leads to suffering."

–Frank Oz as Yoda in *Star Wars: Episode I - The Phantom Menace* (1999)

"Fear can't be trusted."

–Idina Menzel as Elsa in *Frozen 2* (2019)

"Fear of a name only increases fear of the thing itself."

–Emma Watson as Hermione Granger in *Harry Potter and the Chamber of Secrets* (2002)

---

[12] Dallin H. Oaks, "Love Your Enemies," October 2020 General Conference.

[13] Gordon B. Hinckley, "God Hath Not Given Us the Spirit of Fear," *Ensign*, October 1984.

[14] 2 Timothy 1:7

"Never let the fear of striking out keep you from playing the game."

–Whip Hubley as Sam's Dad in *A Cinderella Story* (2004)

"We walk away from our dreams afraid we may fail, or worse yet, afraid we may succeed."

–Sean Connery as William Forrester in *Finding Forrester* (2000)

"What you really fear is inside yourself. You fear your own power. You fear your anger, the drive to do great or terrible things."

–Michael Caine as Alfred Pennyworth in *Batman Begins* (2005)

"You can be too old for a lot of things, but you're never too old to be afraid."

–Roberts Blossom as Marley in *Home Alone* (1990)

"The God of War is our enemy. But his wrath can be quenched with peace, and his anger with love."

–Connie Nielsen as Hippolyta, Queen of the Amazons in *Wonder Woman* (2017)

"There's always something you can do with the mad you feel."

–Tom Hanks as Fred Rogers in *A Beautiful Day in the Neighborhood* (2019)

"Well, you should learn to control your temper!"
–Paige O'Hara as Belle in *Beauty and the Beast* (1991)

"Don't let the haters stop you from doing your thang."
–Rajiv Surendra as Kevin Gnapoor in *Mean Girls* (2004)

"Don't give in to hate. That leads to the Dark Side."
–Alec Guinness as Obi-Wan Kenobi in *Star Wars: Episode V - The Empire Strikes Back* (1980)

Overcoming Adversity

Despite the darkness in the world and in our lives, with the Savior's help and believing His words with faith and hope, we can overcome all things. "There is no darkness so dense, so menacing, or so difficult that it cannot be overcome by light," said Elder Vern P. Stanfill of the Seventy.[15] Elder Soares shared this confidence. "We will win the daily battles against evil, and, rather than fall on the battlefields of life, we will rally others to the Master's standards," the apostle said.[16] Goodness will triumph and righteousness will win in the end. We can each use our individual trials to become better.

Of the many quotes by church leaders, one that has been particularly powerful for me personally when going through

---

[15] Vern P. Stanfill, "Choose the Light," October 2015 General Conference.
[16] Ulisses Soares, "Yes, We Can and Will Win!" April 2015 General Conference.

hard times in life is this one by President Monson. It matches well the spirit of this group of church and movie quotes about overcoming adversity:

> Our Heavenly Father, who gives us so much to delight in, also knows that we learn and grow and become stronger as we face and survive the trials through which we must pass. We know that there are times when we will experience heartbreaking sorrow, when we will grieve, and when we may be tested to our limits. However, such difficulties allow us to change for the better, to rebuild our lives in the way our Heavenly Father teaches us, and to become something different from what we were—better than we were, more understanding than we were, more empathetic than we were, with stronger testimonies than we had before.[17]

"I know bad things happen. Bad things happen. But you can still live. You can still live."

–Joel Courtney as Joe Lamb in *Super 8* (2011)

"Things always get worse before they get better."

–Michael Caine as Alfred Pennyworth in *The Dark Knight* (2008)

"The flower that blooms in adversity is the most rare and beautiful of all."

–Soon-Tek Oh as Fa Zhou in *Mulan* (1998)

---

[17] Thomas S. Monson, "I Will Not Fail Thee, nor Forsake Thee," October 2013 General Conference.

"Everything is a blessing. Even curses are blessings in disguise."

–Kevin Spacey as Eugene Simonet in *Pay It Forward* (2000)

"The very things that held you down are going to lift you up and up and up!"

–Edward Brophy as Timothy Q. Mouse in *Dumbo* (1941)

"In the night, find the light, Rey."

–Olivia d'Abo as Luminara Unduli in *Star Wars: Episode IX - The Rise of Skywalker* (2019)

"Don't be so arrogant to think God can't work through your failures."

–Julia Campbell as Kay Smith in *Jesus Revolution* (2023)

"Let me tell you, at the lowest points of my life I've tried it both ways: doing everything I can to connect to God, or walking away. And in my experience, one feels a whole lot better than the other."

–John Carroll Lynch as Pastor Scott in *Miracles from Heaven* (2016)

"To defeat the darkness out there, you must defeat the darkness inside yourself."

–Bille Brown as Coriakin in *The Chronicles of Narnia: The Voyage of the Dawn Treader* (2010)

"Even though you're bigger than me, you can't win, 'cause you're bad, and the good always wins over the bad."

–Robin Williams as Popeye in *Popeye* (1980)

"After a while, you learn to ignore the names people call you and just trust who you are."

–Mike Myers as Shrek in *Shrek* (2001)

"The problem is not the problem. The problem is your attitude about the problem. Do you understand?"

–Johnny Depp as Jack Sparrow in *Pirates of the Caribbean: The Curse of the Black Pearl* (2003)

"It's not until you lose everything that you truly appreciate everything."

–Paige O'Hara as Belle in *Beauty and the Beast* (1991)

"It's only stuff, Clark. it can always be replaced."

–Diane Lane as Martha Kent as *Man of Steel* (2013)

"It's not about how much we lost. It's about how much we have left."

–Robert Downey Jr. as Tony Stark in *Avengers: Endgame* (2019)

"It's only a passing thing, this shadow. Even darkness must pass. A new day will come. And when the sun shines it will shine out the clearer."

–Sean Astin as Samwise Gamgee in *The Lord of the Rings: The Two Towers* (2002)

16

MISTAKES, REPENTANCE, & FORGIVENESS

The New Testament instructs us that "all have sinned, and come short of the glory of God."[1] As such, we are all commanded to repent and sin no more. Believe it or not, but the movies have a lot of wisdom to share about the gift of repentance, learning from our mistakes, and embarking on a fresh start. Church teachings and movie lines alike warn us that while forgiving others can be difficult, it is worth it and liberating.

The Gift of Repentance

President Uchtdorf sounded a whole lot like Bruce Wayne's butler when he said, "Our destiny is not determined by the number of times we stumble but by the number of times we rise up, dust ourselves off, and move forward." He said, "No matter how many times you have slipped or fallen, rise up!"[2] The gift of repentance is real, and thanks to a loving Savior, we are only a lost sheep, never a lost cause!

Elder Allen D. Haynie of the Seventy sounded like Ryan Reynolds in *Spirited* when he said, "The Savior will never turn away from us when we humbly seek Him in order to repent; will never consider us to be a lost cause."[3] Some of the best movies encourage us to likewise never give up, but instead to pick ourselves up.

---

[1] Romans 3:23

[2] Dieter F. Uchtdorf, "You Can Do It Now!" October 2013 General Conference.

[3] Allen D. Haynie, "Remembering in Whom We Have Trusted," October 2015 General Conference.

"Why do we fall sir? So that we can learn to pick ourselves up."
–Michael Caine as Alfred Pennyworth in *Batman Begins* (2005)

"Just because you're hurt doesn't mean you're broken."
–Morgan Freeman as Dr. Cameron McCarthy in *Dolphin Tale* (2011)

"Even if you lost your way, you don't have to stay a lost cause."
–Ryan Reynolds as Clint Briggs as *Spirited* (2022)

"You know, you don't throw a whole life away just 'cause he's banged up a little."
–Chris Cooper as Tom Smith in *Seabiscuit* (2003)

"I know what I have to do. But going back means I'll have to face my past. I've been running from it for so long."
–Matthew Broderick as Simba in *The Lion King* (1994)

"You want to get out of the hole? First you're going to have to put down the shovel."
–Jonathan Banks as Rick Dicker in *Incredibles 2* (2018)

"God will forgive me. It's His job."
–Brad Pitt as Heinrich Harrer in *Seven Years in Tibet* (1997)

"If you feel like you're an outcast, join us here. If you feel like you're misunderstood and judged, this is where you belong. If you feel ashamed or trapped in something you've done or are doing, you find forgiveness and freedom right here. No guilt trips!"

–Kelsey Grammer as Pastor Chuck Smith in *Jesus Revolution* (2023)

Learn from Mistakes

Since Jesus was the only perfect one to walk the earth, we are all going to come up short sometimes. "Because we are all mortal, we all make mistakes," declared Sister Julie B. Beck of the Young Women General Presidency. "Repentance is not optional, but we don't do it alone. We have a Savior to help us repent."[4] But it's hard to learn from our mistakes, and humbling to reach out for help. "Growth means growing pains," pointed out Elder Hafen. "It also means learning from our mistakes in a continual process made possible by the Savior's grace."[5] Hollywood is filled with imperfect characters, but some give us helpful advice about learning from our mistakes.

"Oh yes, the past can hurt. But you can either run from it, or learn from it."

–Robert Guillaume as Rafiki in *The Lion King* (1994)

---

[4] Julie B. Beck, "Remembering, Repenting, and Changing," April 2007 General Conference.

[5] Bruce C. Hafen, "The Atonement: All for All," April 2004 General Conference.

"It's been proven by history: all mankind makes mistakes."
–Bruce Willis as Captain Sharp in *Moonrise Kingdom* (2012)

"There is a benefit to losing, you get to learn from your mistakes."
–Will Ferrell as Megamind in *Megamind* (2010)

"People make bad choices if they're mad or scared or stressed…Everyone's a bit of a fixer upper."
–Ciarán Hinds as Pabbie/Grandpa in *Frozen* (2013)

"God has a long history of working through flawed people."
–Kelsey Grammer as Pastor Chuck Smith in *Jesus Revolution* (2023)

"You are strong because you are imperfect. You are wise because you have doubts."
–Kristin Scott Thomas as Clemmie Churchill in *Darkest Hour* (2017)

"A pilot never stops acquiring knowledge. You'll make mistakes, everyone does. Just learn from them."
–Jeff Kober as Lt. Cook in *Sully* (2016)

"Because if I hadn't have made them (mistakes), I wouldn't have learned how to make things right."
–Kathy Baker as Beverly Rink in *13 Going on 30* (2004)

"He may have been down, but he wasn't out. He may have lost a few, but he didn't let it get to him. I think I learned a lick or two from this little guy."

–Jeff Bridges as Charles Howard in *Seabiscuit* (2003)

"We must never stop failing, because the minute we do, we've failed."

–Chris Pine as Edgin in *Dungeons & Dragons: Honor Among Thieves* (2023)

"Children need to know that even when adults make plans, sometimes they don't turn out as they hoped."

–Tom Hanks as Fred Rogers in *A Beautiful Day in the Neighborhood* (2019)

"A wise man once said: 'There are no perfect men in the world; only perfect intentions.'"

–Morgan Freeman as Azeem in *Robin Hood: Prince of Thieves* (1991)

Fresh Starts

After we stop digging, and repent and turn our life around, we need the courage to let go of the past and engage in a fresh start. Perhaps he wasn't as sensational as *Frozen*'s Elsa, but Elder Holland also encouraged us to let it go. "I plead with you not to dwell on days now gone nor to yearn vainly for yesterdays, however good those yesterdays may have been," he said. "The past is to be learned from but not lived in."[6] As we let the past die and move into a bright new future, we are allowing ourselves to make a fresh start–beyond the sin and mistakes of yesterday. "There is something incredibly hopeful about a fresh start," said President Uchtdorf. "I suppose at one time or another we have all wanted to start again with a clean slate."[7]

"The past is in the past. Let it go, let it go."
–Idina Menzel as Elsa in *Frozen* (2013)

"Let the past die. Kill it, if you have to. That's the only way to become what you were meant to be."
–Adam Driver as Kylo Ren in *Star Wars: Episode VIII - The Last Jedi* (2017)

"You got to put your behind in your past!"
–Ernie Sabella as Pumbaa in *The Lion King* (1994)

"I never look back, darling. It distracts from the now."
–Brad Bird as Edna Mode in *The Incredibles* (2004)

"All we can do is our best, and sometimes the best that we can do is to start over."
–Hayley Atwell as Peggy Carter in *Captain America: The First Avenger* (2011)

---

[6] Jeffrey R. Holland, "The Best Is Yet to Be," *BYU Speeches,* 13 January 2009.
[7] Dieter F. Uchtdorf, "The Best Time to Plant a Tree," *Ensign*, January 2014.

"Just because someone stumbles and loses their path, doesn't mean they're lost forever."

–Patrick Stewart as Professor X in *X-Men: Days of Future Past* (2014)

"For what it's worth: it's never too late or, in my case, too early to be whoever you want to be. . . I hope you live a life a life you're proud of. If you find that you're not, I hope you have the strength to start all over again."

–Brad Pitt as Benjamin Button in *The Curious Case of Benjamin Button* (2008)

"Our greatest glory is not in ever falling, but in rising every time we fall."

–Christain Bale as Batman in *The Dark Knight* (2008)

Brooke: "You never let anything get to you. How do you do that?"
Grace: "Jesus."

–Hayley Orrantia as Brooke Thawley and Melissa Joan Hart as Grace Wesley in *God's Not Dead 2* (2016)

Forgiveness is Difficult

The Lord is quick to forgive us. "Yea, and as often as my people repent will I forgive them their trespasses against me," we read in the Book of Mormon.[8] But most of us mortals struggle with

8 Mosiah 26:30

the Christlike ability to forgive. "I am convinced that most of us want to forgive, but we find it very hard to do," said Elder Kevin R. Duncan of the Seventy. "If you are having trouble forgiving another person or even yourself, ask God to help you. Forgiveness is a glorious, healing principle. We do not need to be a victim twice. We can forgive," he said.[9] Yet, despite its difficulty, we are commanded to forgive aggressively. "I, the Lord, will forgive whom I will forgive, but of you it is required to forgive all men," reads the scripture.[10] This, as some films point out, includes forgiving those who are right, those we love, and even ourselves.

"Dumbledore says people find it far easier to forgive others for being wrong than being right."

–Emma Watson as Hermione Granger in *Harry Potter and the Half-Blood Prince* (2009)

"It's strange, but sometimes it's hardest of all to forgive someone we love."

–Tom Hanks as Fred Rogers in *A Beautiful Day in the Neighborhood* (2019)

"You can be as mad as a mad dog at the way things went. You could swear, curse the fates, but when it comes to the end, you have to let go."

–Brad Pitt as Benjamin Button in *The Curious Case of Benjamin Button* (2008)

---

[9] Kevin R. Duncan, "The Healing Ointment of Forgiveness," April 2016 General Conference.

[10] D&C 64:10

"To err is human, to forgive divine."

–Maggie Smith as Mother Superior in *Sister Act* (1992)

"Good people end up in hell because they can't forgive themselves."

–Robin Williams as Chris Nielsen in *What Dreams May Come* (1998)

"Atlanteans are many wonderful things, but forgiving is not one of them."

–Amber Heard as Mera in *Aquaman* (2018)

Forgiveness is Liberating

Forgiving others, as difficult as it may seem, can be one of the most liberating and Christlike things we do. "When we forgive others, it frees us to choose how we will live our own lives," said Elder David E. Sorensen of the Seventy. "Forgiveness means that problems of the past no longer dictate our destinies, and we can focus on the future with God's love in our hearts."[11] What a wonderful thing! Instead of chasing after an offending rattlesnake and dying of poison along the way, we can purge ourselves of the venom through forgiveness and move on. "Even though we may be a victim once, we need not be a victim twice by carrying the burden of hate, bitterness, pain,

[11] David E. Sorensen, "Forgiveness Will Change Bitterness to Love," April 2003 General Conference.

resentment, or even revenge," added Elder Duncan. "We can forgive, and we can be free!"[12]

"Forgiveness liberates the soul. It removes fear. That is why it is such a powerful weapon."

–Morgan Freeman as Nelson Mandela in *Invictus* (2009)

"For man with no forgiveness in heart, life worse punishment than death."

–Pat Morita as Mr. Miyagi in *The Karate Kid* (1984)

"Do you know what forgiveness means? It's a decision we make to release a person from the feelings of anger we have against them. Depression is rage turned inward. Forgive is to release the anger for someone or something."

–Tom Hanks as Fred Rogers in *A Beautiful Day in the Neighborhood* (2019)

"Forgiveness doesn't have to wait. I'm free to forgive myself and so are you. It's a beautiful thing. It really is."

–John Carroll Lynch as Pruitt in *The Invitation* (2022)

"I don't even remember what it was I was mad about and I don't care. Whatever it was that you did, I forgive you."

–Barbara Hershey as Hillary Whitney Essex in *Beaches* (1988)

---

[12] Kevin R. Duncan, "The Healing Ointment of Forgiveness," April 2016 General Conference.

17

VALIANT, PERSISTENT, & STRONG

The Primary children sing about the Lord needing valiant servants, and indeed He does. To be enlisted until the conflict is over among the ranks of marching Christian soldiers, we must be among those who will work and problem solve. We need to persevere with courage and valor. We must be valiant, persistent, and strong to successfully defeat the Dark Side!

Work and Problem Solving

Work and industry have been essential to living the temporal gospel–there is a reason why Utah's symbol is the beehive and the state motto is "Industry." God would have us be constructive. "To work—honestly and productively—brings contentment and a sense of self-worth," taught Presiding Bishop H. David Burton.[1] "Work is the means to achieve happiness, prosperity, and salvation," said Bishop J. Richard Clarke. "When work and duty and joy are commingled, then man is at his best."[2] The hymn reminds us that "we all have work, let no one shirk."[3]

Likewise, many movies glorify the hard worker and deride the slacker. "There is no room for a slacker, a critic, a pessimist, concerning this the work of the Almighty," said President Hinckley.[4] *Back to the Future*'s Mr. Strickland has no patience for slackers, either. There is also merit in not just working harder, but working smarter, as Scrooge McDuck would remind

[1] H. David Burton, "The Blessing of Work," *Liahona*, December 2009.
[2] J. Richard Clarke, "The Value of Work," April 1992 General Conference.
[3] Hymn 252, "Put Your Shoulder to the Wheel."
[4] Gordon B. Hinckley, "A Conversation with Single Adults," *Ensign*, March 1997.

his nephews, and some films brilliantly encourage problem solving, too.

"The only way to get what you want in this world is through hard work."

–Anika Noni Rose as Tiana in *The Princess and the Frog* (2009)

"My mind rebels at stagnation. Give me problems, give me work."

–Robert Downey, Jr. as Sherlock Holmes in *Sherlock Holmes* (2009)

"You can praise God by peeling a spud if you peel it to perfection."

–John Young as Reverend J.D. Liddell in *Chariots of Fire* (1981)

"In every job that must be done, there is an element of fun. You find the fun, and — SNAP — the job's a game!"

–Julie Andrews as Mary Poppins in *Mary Poppins* (1964)

"If you've ever seen the look on somebody's face the day they finally get a job--I've had some experience with this, they look like they could fly. And it's not about the paycheck, it's about respect; it's about looking in the mirror and knowing that you've done something valuable with your day."

–Kevin Kline as Dave Kovic in *Dave* (1993)

"We can't take any credit for our talents. It's how we use them that counts."

–Reese Witherspoon as Mrs. Whatsit in *A Wrinkle in Time* (2018)

"You got a real attitude problem, McFly; you're a slacker. You remind me of your father when he went here; he was a slacker, too."

–James Tolkan as Mr. Strickland in *Back to the Future* (1985)

"I don't need easy. I just need possible."

–AnnaSophia Robb as Bethany Hamilton in *Soul Surfer* (2011)

"I have nothing to offer but blood, toil, tears and sweat."

–Gary Oldman as Winston Churchill in *Darkest Hour* (2017)

"How many times do I have to teach you: just because something works doesn't mean it can't be improved."

–Letitia Wright as Shuri in *Black Panther* (2018)

"If you put your mind to it, you can accomplish anything."

–Michael J. Fox as Marty McFly in *Back to the Future* (1985)

"When something is too hard… there is always another way."

–Eugene Levy as Charlie in *Finding Dory* (2016)

Perseverance

In the quest for a righteous and joyful life, we must be persistent and be Saints that press forward. President Faust taught us, "Perseverance is demonstrated by those who keep going when the going gets tough, who don't give up even when others say, 'It can't be done.'"[5] Great films encourage us to persevere through trials, too. "We must never give up, regardless of temptations, frustrations, disappointments, or discouragements," said Elder Wirthlin. "I believe that perseverance is vital to success in any endeavor, whether spiritual or temporal, large or small, public or personal."[6]

After all, some missions are too vital to give up on. "When doing the Lord's work, failure is not an option," pointed out Elder Sterling W. Sill.[7] So what do we do when the going gets tough? Elder J. Christopher Lansing (tapping into Dory, a blue fish with a bad memory) taught, "Obstacles come into each of our lives, but to get through them and to get where we want to go, we must keep swimming."[8]

"Failure is not an option."

–Ed Harris as Gene Kranz in *Apollo 13* (1995)

"Marty, one rejection isn't the end of the world."

–Claudia Wells as Jennifer Parker in *Back to the Future* (1985)

---

[5] James E. Faust, "Perseverance," April 2005 General Conference.

[6] Joseph B. Wirthlin, "Never Give Up," October 1987 General Conference.

[7] Sterling W. Sill, "Creative Leadership in a Changing World," *BYU Speeches*, 14 June 1961.

[8] J. Christopher Lansing, "Enduring Well," *Liahona*, January 2014.

"Never give up because you never know what the tide will bring in the next day."

–Tom Hanks as Chuck Noland in *Cast Away* (2000)

"Two little mice fell in a bucket of cream. The first mouse quickly gave up and drowned. The second mouse wouldn't quit. He struggled so hard that eventually he churned that cream into butter and crawled out."

–Christopher Walken as Frank Abignale, Sr. in *Catch Me If You Can* (2002)

"Just keep swimming. Just keep swimming. Just keep swimming, swimming, swimming. What do we do? We swim, swim."

–Ellen DeGeneres as Dory in *Finding Nemo* (2003)

"Never give up; never surrender!"

–Tim Allen as Jason Nesmith in *Galaxy Quest* (1999)

"Everything's impossible until somebody does it."

–Christian Bale as Bruce Wayne in *The Dark Knight Rises* (2012)

"No cause is lost if but one fool is left to fight for it."

–Orlando Bloom as Will Turner in *Pirates of the Caribbean: Dead Man's Chest* (2006)

"Promise me, you'll survive. That you won't give up, no matter what happens. No matter how hopeless, promise Rose and never let go of that promise."

–Leonardo DiCaprio as Jack Dawson in *Titanic* (1997)

"Never give up and good luck will find you."

–Alan Oppenheimer as Falcor in *The NeverEnding Story* (1984)

"Nothing's impossible, Charlie."

–Liz Smith as Grandma Georgina in *Charlie and the Chocolate Factory* (2005)

"Sometimes, a winner is a dreamer who just won't quit."

–Sean Astin as Daniel E. 'Rudy' Ruettiger in *Rudy* (1993)

Courage

Living the gospel of Jesus Christ requires us to also be courageous. "Let us be confident, not apologetic, valiant, not timid, faithful, not fearful as we hold up the Lord's light in these last days," said Elder Jörg Klebingat of the Seventy.[9] Sometimes we need to summon the courage to move forward and sometimes life requires the courage to stand for what we believe in and be immovable. "May we muster courage at the

---

[9] Jörg Klebingat, "Valiant Discipleship in the Latter Days," April 2022 General Conference.

crossroads, courage for the conflicts, courage to say no, courage to say yes, for courage counts," declared President Monson.[10]

It takes courage to face our fears, too, but it is worth it. "All men have their fears, but those who face their fears with dignity have courage as well," President Monson said.[11] Actors in the big pictures, from talking candlesticks to heroes, advise us to take courage, too.

"You don't have time to be timid. You must be bold, daring."
–Jerry Orbach as Lumiere in *Beauty and the Beast* (1991)

"The things you're scared of are usually the most worthwhile."
–Mandy Moore as Anna Foster in *Chasing Liberty* (2004)

"There is no courage without fear."
–Soon-Tek Oh as Fa Zhou in *Mulan* (1998)

"Courage is not the absence of fear, but rather the judgment that something is more important than fear. The brave may not live forever, but the cautious do not live at all."
–Rene Auberjonois as Philippe Renaldi, Prince of Genovia in *The Princess Diaries: The Royal Engagement* (2004)

---

[10] Thomas S. Monson, "Courage Counts," October 1986 General Conference.
[11] Thomas S. Monson, "The Call for Courage," April 2004 General Conference.

“Success is not final, failure is not fatal, it is the courage to continue that counts.”

–Gary Oldman as Winston Churchill in *Darkest Hour* (2017)

“You are braver than you believe, stronger than you seem, and smarter than you think.”

–Brady Bluhm as Christopher Robin in *Pooh’s Grand Adventure: The Search for Christopher Robin* (1997)

“I've seen knights in armor panic at the first hint of battle. And I've seen the lowliest, unarmed squire pull a spear from his own body, to defend a dying horse. Nobility is not a birthright. It's defined by one's actions.”

–Kevin Costner as Robin Hood in *Robin Hood: Prince of Thieves* (1991)

“Compromise where you can. Where you can’t, don’t. Even if everyone is telling you that something wrong is something right. Even if the whole world is telling you to move, it is your duty to plant yourself like a tree, look them in the eye, and say, ‘No, you move.'”

–Emily VanCamp as Sharon Carter in *Captain America: Civil War* (2016)

“No matter how the wind howls, the mountain cannot bow to it.”

–Pat Morita as Emperor in *Mulan* (1998)

"It's not easy to stand alone against the ridicule of others."

–Joseph Sweeney as Juror #9 in *12 Angry Men* (1957)

"We can be heroes in our own lives, every one of us, if we only have the courage to try."

–Peter Cullen as Optimus Prime in *Transformers: The Last Knight* (2017)

"Oh, you only fight the fights you can win? You fight the fights that need fighting!"

–Martin Sheen as A. J. MacInerney in *The American President* (1995)

"Sometimes all you need is twenty seconds of insane courage. Just literally twenty seconds of just embarrassing bravery. And I promise you, something great will come of it."

–Matt Damon as Benjamin Mee in *We Bought a Zoo* (2011)

"Courage! What makes a king out of a slave? Courage! What makes the flag on the mast to wave? Courage! What makes the elephant charge his tusk in the misty mist, or the dusky dusk? What makes the muskrat guard his musk? Courage! What makes the sphinx the seventh wonder? Courage! What makes the dawn come up like thunder? Courage! What makes the Hottentot so hot? What puts the 'ape' in apricot? What have they got that I ain't got?"

–Bert Lahr as The Cowardly Lion in *The Wizard of Oz* (1939)

Valor

A special type of courage is valor–this is the greatest of courage; the courage needed in the heat of battle; the courage needed to get up again after suffering defeat. "Even when you fail, you can choose not to give up, but rather discover your courage, press forward, and rise up," advised President Uchtdorf.[12] Elder Wirthlin put it this way; "Sometimes we get discouraged and feel like giving up. But, as an old cowboy once said, 'If I get bucked off, I must get back up on the horse and ride on.' We can never give up."[13]

Many films describe the triumph of sports and getting up again after getting knocked down. "Anyone seeking success in athletics or in life must have two qualities. Number one, he must have the ability to give a big punch, and number two, he must have the ability to take a big punch," said Elder Sill of this valor. "Now sometimes in our lives we take great pride in how we can hand it out, but then we go down in a miserable heap because we can't take it."[14]

"Take all the bruises, but stay in the ring."

–Jimmy Smits as Kevin Rosario in *In the Heights* (2021)

---

[12] Dieter F. Uchtdorf, "Your Great Adventure," October 2019 General Conference.

[13] Joseph B. Wirthlin, "Spiritually Strong Homes and Families," April 1993 General Conference.

[14] Sterling W. Sill, "Transfusion," October 1974 General Conference.

"You know what separates the winners from the losers? Getting back on the horse after being kicked in the teeth."

–Gene Hackman as Jimmy McGinty in *The Replacements* (2000)

"It ain't about how hard you hit. It's about how hard you can get hit and keep moving forward; how much you can take and keep moving forward. That's how winning is done!"

–Sylvester Stallone as Rocky Balboa in *Rocky Balboa* (2006)

"You wanna be really great? Then have the courage to fail big and stick around. Make them wonder why you're still smiling."

–Kirsten Dunst as Claire Colburn in *Elizabethtown* (2005)

"This is my fight. Everyone's got one."

–Sean Farris as Jake Tyler in *Never Back Down* (2008)

"I choose to run towards my problems, and not away from them. Because that–because that's what heroes do."

–Chris Hemsworth as Thor in *Thor: Ragnarok* (2017)

"Loyalty, honor, a willing heart. I can ask no more than that."

–Richard Armitage as Thorin Oakenshield in *The Hobbit: An Unexpected Journey* (2012)

"No man can win every battle, but no man should fall without a struggle."

–Tom Holland as Peter Parker in *Spider-Man: Homecoming* (2019)

"We're warriors who serve the good and light in the universe."

–Reese Witherspoon as Mrs. Whatsit in *A Wrinkle in Time* (2018)

18

TAKING ACTION TODAY

Some of the best movies are action flicks, and some of the best lives are filled with action and not mere talk. Sadly in life, after all is said and done, there is more that is said than done! Both great Hollywood films and great latter-day teachings nudge us to do something, to seize the potential of each day, and to savor and maximize the opportunities in each moment. We can be women and men of action and doing good.

Do Something!

The gospel has always been a plan of action. "Being a disciple of Jesus Christ involves more than just hoping or believing," pointed out Sister Rebecca L. Craven of the Young Women General Presidency. "It calls for effort, movement, and commitment. It requires that we do something, being 'doers of the word, and not hearers only.'"[1] Wizards and Jedi, along with prophets and apostles, encourage us to take action and DO IT.

"Discipleship is not a spectator sport," said President Uchtdorf. "We cannot expect to experience the blessings of faith by standing inactive on the sidelines."[2] We sing that we should "wake up and do something more," and indeed we should![3] President Nelson said, "We need to get up off the couch, put down the remote, and wake up from our spiritual slumber. It is time to put on the full armor of God so we can engage in the

---

[1] Rebecca L. Craven, "Do What Mattereth Most," April 2022 General Conference.

[2] Dieter F. Uchtdorf, "The Way of the Disciple," April 2009 General Conference.

[3] Hymn 223, "Have I Done Any Good?"

most important work on earth."[4] The call to action continues in our favorite flicks.

"If you never do anything, you never become anyone."
–Carey Mulligan as Jenny Mellor in *An Education* (2009)

"In the end, it is not important what you think. It is only important what you do."
–Liam Neeson as The Monster in *A Monster Calls* (2016)

"It does not do well to dwell on dreams and forget to live."
–Richard Harris as Albus Dumbledore in *Harry Potter and the Sorcerer's Stone* (2001)

"Life's not a spectator sport. If watchin' is all you're gonna do, then you're gonna watch your life go by without ya."
–Mary Wickes as Laverne in *The Hunchback of Notre Dame* (1996)

"Do, or do not. There is no 'try'."
–Frank Oz as Yoda in *Star Wars: Episode V - The Empire Strikes Back* (1980)

"The brave may not live forever, but the cautious do not live at all."
–Rene Auberjonois as Phillipe Renaldi in *The Princess Diaries* (2001)

---

[4] Russell M. Nelson, "We Can Do Better and Be Better," April 2019 General Conference.

"I don't want to survive. I want to live."
–Jeff Garlin as Captain in *WALL-E* (2008)

"Sooner or later, though, you always have to wake up."
–Sam Worthington as Jake Sully in *Avatar* (2009)

"I have to do something."
–Ming-Na Wen as Mulan in *Mulan* (1998)

"Don't just stand there, do something!"
–Ursula Reit as Mrs. Gloop in *Willy Wonka & the Chocolate Factory* (1971)

"Don't let anyone ever make you feel like you don't deserve what you want. Go for it."
–Heath Ledger as Patrick in *10 Things I Hate About You* (1999)

"We're Americans. We don't plan, we do!"
–Bill Hader as General George Armstrong Custer in *Night at the Museum: Battle of the Smithsonian* (2009)

"We work with what we got, right?"
–Don Cheadle as James Rhodes in *Avengers: Endgame* (2019)

Seize Each Day

Not only must we act on living a good life, but we must act TODAY! "Daydreaming of the past and longing for the future may provide comfort but will not take the place of living in the present," advised President Monson. "This is the day of our opportunity, and we must grasp it."[5] Sister Sharon Eubank of the Relief Society General Presidency was right when she said, "This is your day, this is your time."[6] Hollywood films remind us to seize the day, and also that tiny actions by each of us today can tip the scales for good. "Your strong voice is needed," similarly said President Hinckley. "The weight of your stance may be enough to tip the scales in the direction of truth."[7]

"Carpe diem. Seize the day, boys. Make your lives extraordinary."

–Robin Williams as John Keating in *Dead Poets Society* (1989)

"Yesterday is history, tomorrow is a mystery, but today is a gift. That's why we call it the present."

–Randall Duk Kim as Master Oogway in *Kung Fu Panda* (2008)

"Begin each day like it was on purpose."

–Will Smith as Alex Hitchens in *Hitch* (2005)

---

[5] Thomas S. Monson, "In Search of Treasure," April 2003 General Conference.

[6] Sharon Eubank, "Turn On Your Light," October 2017 General Conference.

[7] Gordon B. Hinckley, "Stand Up for Truth," *BYU Speeches*, 17 September 1996.

"You were meant to be here tonight. This is your time."

–Kurt Russell as Herb Brooks in *Miracle* (2004)

"Today is a good day to try."

–Tom Hulce as Quasimodo in *The Hunchback of Notre Dame* (1996)

"A single grain of rice can tip the scale. One man may be the difference between victory and defeat."

–Pat Morita as Emperor in *Mulan* (1998)

"Even the tiniest of actions can change the future."

–Britt Robertson as Casey Newton in *Tomorrowland* (2015)

"Honey, time marches on and eventually you realize it's marchin' across your face."

–Dolly Parton as Truvy in *Steel Magnolias* (1989)

"I can't freeze this moment, but I can still go out and seize this day."

–Idina Menzel as Elsa in *Frozen 2* (2019)

Improve the Shining Moments

Even more specific than acting today is acting in this very moment. Cherish the moments of life. Make them count! President Monson was a champion of encouraging us to make the most of today's moments. "There is no tomorrow to remember if we don't do something today," he once said.

"Rather than dwelling on the past, we should make the most of today, of the here and now, doing all we can to provide pleasant memories for the future." He then said, "Opportunities come, and then they are gone. I plead with you not to let those most important things pass you by as you plan for that illusive and nonexistent future when you will have time to do all that you want to do."[8] To this end, we sing "Improve the shining moments; don't let them pass you by." After all, "Time flies on wings of lightning; we cannot call it back."[9] These truths are even espoused in the movies by genies, high school truants, and more!

"Our lives are defined by opportunities, even the ones we miss."
–Brad Pitt as Benjamin Button in *The Curious Case of Benjamin Button* (2008)

"Success doesn't come for free, Miguel. You have to be willing to do whatever it takes to seize your moment."
–Benjamin Bratt as Ernesto de la Cruz in *Coco* (2017)

"You pile up enough tomorrows, and you'll collect nothing but a lot of empty yesterdays."
–Robert Preston as Harold Hill in *The Music Man* (1962)

"Today's special moments are tomorrow's memories."
–Robin Williams as Genie in *Aladdin* (1992)

---

[8] Thomas S. Monson, "Finding Joy in the Journey," October 2008 General Conference.
[9] Hymn 226, "Improve the Shining Moments."

"Fate rarely calls upon us at a moment of our choosing."

–Peter Cullen as Optimus Prime in *Transformers: Revenge of the Fallen* (2009)

"Life is not the amount of breaths you take. It's the moments that take your breath away."

–Will Smith as Alex Hitchens in *Hitch* (2005)

"Life moves pretty fast. If you don't stop and look around once in a while, you could miss it."

–Matthew Broderick as Ferris Bueller in *Ferris Bueller's Day Off* (1986)

"If we didn't do what we loved, we wouldn't exist."

–Michael B. Jordan as Adonis Johnson in *Creed 2* (2018)

Act Now!

President Kimball famously said "DO IT," enthusiastically encouraging us to act now on the good that God would have us do.[10] "We are accountable and will be judged for how we use what we have received," said President Oaks; "to the precious hours and days allotted to each of us during our time in mortality."[11] So let's each sing our song, boldly venture outside our comfort zones, and act to improve our own lives and the lives of those around us. And what are we scared of? Both a great coach in a movie and an apostle of the Lord tell us that it is

---

[10] Quoted in Robert L. Simpson, "Do It," October 1975 General Conference.

[11] Dallin H. Oaks, "Focus and Priorities," April 2001 General Conference.

simply enough to do our best. "This is very important: as we do our best, He will not let us fail," said Apostle Neil L. Anderson.[12]

"Your time is now. So go ahead and sing your song."

–Matthew McConaughey as Buster Moon in *Sing* (2016)

"Fortune favors the bold."

–Tom Hollander as Jim Beach in *Bohemian Rhapsody* (2018)

"What I do know, is that if we do not act soon, it is our children and our grandchildren who will have to pay the price."

–Dennis Quaid as Jack Hall in *The Day After Tomorrow* (2004)

"Venture outside your comfort zone. The rewards are worth it."

–Mandy Moore as Rapunzel in *Tangled* (2010)

"All we have to do is decide what to do with the time that is given to us."

–Ian McKellen as Gandalf in *The Lord of the Rings: The Fellowship of the Ring* (2001)

"No amount of money ever bought a second of time."

–Robert Downey Jr. as Tony Stark in *Avengers: Endgame* (2019)

---

[12] Neil L. Andersen, "A Spiritual Work," *2013 Worldwide Leadership Training.*

"Do your best. That's all anybody can ask for."
–Denzel Washington as Coach Boone in *Remember the Titans* (2000)

"If you were waiting for the opportune moment, that was it."
–Johnny Depp as Jack Sparrow in *Pirates of the Caribbean: The Curse of the Black Pearl* (2003)

"There's a million things I haven't done, just you wait."
–Lin-Manuel Miranda as Alexander Hamilton in *Hamilton* (202

19

DESTINY & POTENTIAL

Many films tell the story of protagonists who grow beyond humble beginnings. There is much talk about one's destiny on the one hand, and an unwritten future on the other. The gospel likewise addresses these themes and helpfully explains to us the nuanced truth that divine destiny is real, but predestination is not; that our future is a blank storyboard, but that God does have big plans for each of us. Dozens of movie quotes help us better understand these truths, too.

Grow Beyond Your Origins

Eternal progression is a critical part of the Father's Plan of Happiness. "In the Lord's timing, it is not where we start but where we are headed that matters most," taught Elder Gilbert. "Our future will be determined far less by our starting point and much more by our slope," he said.[1] Growing from humble beginnings to greatness is also a major theme in motion pictures. This is a gospel truth, too. After all, "who we are is not who we can become," said Elder Donald L. Hallstrom of the Seventy.[2] We must be humble with our aspirations (as Darth Vader reminds us), but we can still aspire to be so much more than we started as! "You can shape who you become, you can be more than you are today," said Elder Andersen.[3]

---

[1] Clark C. Gilbert, "Becoming More in Christ: The Parable of the Slope," October 2021 General Conference.

[2] Donald L. Hallstrom, "What Manner of Men?" April 2014 General Conference.

[3] Neil L. Andersen, "Preparing for Your Spiritual Destiny," *BYU Speeches*, 10 January 2010.

"Big things have small beginnings, sir."

–Claude Rains as Mr. Dryden in *Lawrence of Arabia* (1962)

"It matters not what someone is born, but what they grow to be."

–Michael Gambon as Albus Dumbledore in *Harry Potter and the Goblet of Fire* (2005)

"Your story may not have such a happy beginning but that does not make you who you are, it is the rest of it- who you choose to be."

–Michelle Yeoh as Soothsayer in *Kung Fu Panda 2* (2011)

"It's not about what it is, it's about what it can become."

–Ed Helms as The Once-ler in *The Lorax* (2012)

"You must not let anyone define your limits because of where you come from. Your only limit is your soul."

–Brad Garret as Chef Gusteau in *Ratatouille* (2007)

"Do you think we choose the times into which we are born? Or do we fit the times we are born into?"

–Daniel Day-Lewis as Abraham Lincoln in *Lincoln* (2012)

"Some men are born great, others have greatness thrust upon them."

–Robin Williams as Teddy Roosevelt in *Night at the Museum* (2006)

"I wouldn't presume to tell you what to do with your past, sir. Just know that there are those of us who care about what you do with your future."

–Michael Caine as Alfred Pennyworth in *Batman Begins* (2005)

"Shoot for the moon, kid. Shoot for the moon."

–Alan Arkin as Wild Knuckles in *Minions: The Rise of Gru* (2022)

"Be careful not to choke on your aspirations."

–James Earl Jones as Darth Vader in *Rogue One: A Star Wars Story* (2016)

Destiny Approaches

We believe in destiny. Not in some predestination sort of way, but in a way that means there are certain prophecies that WILL be fulfilled, that there are promises and blessings (along with warnings and cautions) that WILL come to pass. "I am positive in my mind that the Lord has planned our destiny," said President Kimball. "God controls our lives, guides and blesses us, but gives us our agency," he said.[4] President Nelson

[4] Spencer W. Kimball, *Faith Precedes the Miracle*, 102–3.

explained divine destiny this way. "Each day is a day of decision, and our decisions determine our destiny. One day each of us will stand before the Lord in judgment."[5]

"I try to make sense of things. Which is why, I guess, I believe in destiny. There must be a reason that I am as I am. There must be."

–Robin Williams as Andrew Martin in *Bicentennial Man* (1999)

"Dread it, run from it, destiny arrives all the same."

–Josh Brolin as Thanos in *Avengers: Infinity War* (2018)

"I don't know if we each have a destiny, or if we're all just floating around accidental – like on a breeze, but I, I think maybe it's both."

–Tom Hanks as Forrest Gump in *Forrest Gump* (1994)

"You know that everything happens for a reason."

–Jennifer Aniston as Grace in *Bruce Almighty* (2003)

"Your mission, should you choose to accept it, is to face your fate."

–Henry Czerny as Eugene Kittridge in *Mission: Impossible* (1996)

---

[5] Russell M. Nelson, "Decisions for Eternity," October 2013 General Conference.

"It is your destiny. Join me."

–James Earl Jones as Darth Vader in *Star Wars: Episode V - The Empire Strikes Back* (1980)

"Perhaps we've just forgotten that we are still pioneers. And we've barely begun. And that our greatest accomplishments cannot be behind us, because our destiny lies above us."

—Matthew McConaughey as Joseph "Coop" Cooper in *Interstellar* (2014)

"We're in the end game now."

–Benedict Cumberbatch as Dr. Stephen Strange in *Avengers: Infinity War* (2018)

The Future is Unwritten

We know that even though God has great plans for us, we have the agency to choose our own path. "Because of the Restoration and because of a true and fuller understanding of mankind's origin and destiny, we know that we are not predestined to anything," taught Elder Ballard.[6] In fact, "you can be anything you want to be in righteousness," taught Elder Holland.[7] This means that your future is unwritten, and it is up to you to see where the main character in your personal adventure of life will

---

6 Christoffel Golden Jr., "To Know Thee, the Only True God," *BYU Speeches*, 8 February 2011.

7 Jeffrey R. Holland, "For Times of Trouble," *BYU Speeches,* 18 March 1980.

end up. Both movies and church leaders attest to this fact. "You cannot see exactly where your future will lead," said Elder Johnson, "but you can ensure your future happiness by making righteous decisions now."[8] So go forward boldly, with the confidence that your future has not yet been decided!

"For the future is never truly set."

–James McAvoy as Younger Charles Xavier in *X-Men: Days of Future Past* (2014)

"Even the wise cannot see all the ends."

–Ian McKellen as Gandalf in *The Lord of the Rings: The Fellowship of the Ring* (2001)

"It means your future hasn't been written yet, no one's has."

–Christopher Lloyd as Dr. Emmett Brown in *Back to the Future, Part III* (1990)

"Nothing is written."

–Peter O'Toole as T.E. Lawrence in *Lawrence of Arabia* (1962)

"I'm unsure of the future but I'm not concerned. I will rely on those closest to me, and I will share their burdens, as they share mine. I will live and I will love."

–Brad Pitt as Roy McBride in *Ad Astra* (2019)

"You can't hurry the future."

–John Leguizamo as Bruno in *Encanto* (2021)

---

[8] Paul V. Johnson, "Making Righteous Choices," *New Era*, September 2010.

"The soul of man has been given wings and at last he is beginning to fly. He is flying into the rainbow! Into the light of hope, into the future! The glorious future that belongs to you, to me and to all of us."

–Charlie Chaplin as Hynkel - Dictator of Tomania in *The Great Dictator* (1940)

"Go. Live your dream."

–Brad Garrett as Hook Hand in *Tangled* (2010)

YOU Decide Your Destiny

The good news is that WE choose which path to take. WE decide our own destiny. "Remember that YOU are the master of your thoughts," admonished Sister Linda S. Reeves of the Relief Society General Presidency. "Satan cannot force you to do anything you don't want to do. Take control of your life!" she said.[9] The Prophet Nephi saw this as good news, too. "Therefore, cheer up your hearts, and remember that ye are free to act for yourselves—to choose the way of everlasting death or the way of eternal life."[10]

"We all have our agency," reminded President Nelson. "We can choose to let God prevail in our lives, or not. We can choose to let God be the most powerful influence in our lives, or not."[11] Protagonists on the big screen prod us to come to the Light Side.

---

[9] Linda S. Reeves, "You Are the Master of Your Thoughts," *Church News,* 16 July 2015.

[10] 2 Nephi 10:23

[11] Russell M. Nelson, "Let God Prevail," October 2020 General Conference.

"I hope we can always choose the light," said Elder Gerrit W. Gong of the Twelve. "When we are filled with light, we feel happy and peaceful and safe."[12]

"I believe we make our own destiny."
–Jake Gyllenhaal as Prince Dastan in *Prince of Persia: The Sands of Time* (2010)

"They don't make you. You make you."
–Isaac Hempstead Wright as Eggs in *The Boxtrolls* (2014)

"A real man makes his own luck."
–Billy Zane as Cal Hockley in *Titanic* (1997)

"Who do I aspire to be? That's the question we should be asking ourselves all the time."
–Daveed Diggs as Mr. Browne in *Wonder* (2017)

"You control your destiny – you don't need magic to do it. And there are no magical shortcuts to solving your problems."
–Kelly Macdonald as Merida in *Brave* (2012)

"You are who you choose to be."
–Eli Marienthal as Hogarth Hughes in *The Iron Giant* (1999)

"We are who we choose to be. Now...choose!"
–Willem Dafoe as Green Goblin in *Spider-Man* (2002)

[12] Gerrit W. Gong, "Choose the Light," *Liahona*, March 2012.

"You need to learn how to select your thoughts just the same way you select your clothes every day. This is a power you can cultivate. If you want to control things in your life so bad, work on the mind. That's the only thing you should be trying to control."

–Richard Jenkins as Richard in *Eat, Pray, Love* (2010)

"We've all got both light and dark inside us. What matters is the part we choose to act on. That's who we really are."

–Gary Oldman as Sirius Black in *Harry Potter and the Order of the Phoenix* (2007)

"I'll never turn to the dark side."

–Mark Hamill as Luke Skywalker in *Star Wars: Episode VI - Return of the Jedi* (1983)

"History has its eyes on you."

–Christopher Jackson as George Washington in *Hamilton* (2020)

God Has Plans for You

Even though our future is unwritten, we have a tremendous opportunity to measure up to the grand plans our loving Heavenly Parents have for each of us. "God will help you become something greater than you ever thought possible," taught President Uchtdorf.[13] In fact, God's plans for you may even exceed your grandest dreams. "He has big plans for you, but don't be surprised if His plans aren't exactly the same as the plans you have made for yourself," said Elder Craig C. Christensen of the Seventy. "Our Heavenly Father sees more in you than you see in yourself, and His vision for you is greater than you can even imagine."[14] May the wise movie quotes and true doctrine taught in this collection inspire you to find the path God would have you go down and may you rise to meet your celestial destiny and potential!

"Maybe God has a bigger plan for me than I had for myself."

–Mandy Moore as Jamie Sullivan in *A Walk to Remember* (2002)

"Maybe God has chosen something bigger for me. Something I wouldn't have chosen for myself."

–Britt Robertson as Melissa in *I Still Believe* (2020)

"I had my eyes opened. I came to realize that I had more to offer this world than just making things that blow up."

–Robert Downey Jr. as Tony Stark in *Iron Man* (2008)

"You mustn't be afraid to dream a little bigger, darling."

–Tom Hardy as Eames in *Inception* (2010)

---

13 Dieter F. Uchtdorf, "It Works Wonderfully!" October 2015 General Conference.

14 Quoted in Marianne Holman Prescott, "Trust God and Do Anything, BYU–Hawaii Graduates Told," *Church News*, 17 April 2014.

"Things we lose have a way of coming back to us in the end, if not always in the way we expect."

–Evanna Lynch as Luna Lovegood in *Harry Potter and the Order of the Phoenix* (2007)

"You know your path, child, now follow it."

–Linda Hunt as Grandmother Willow in *Pocahontas* (1995)

THE END

"And to the reader I bid farewell, hoping that many of my brethren may read my words. Brethren, adieu."
–Jacob 7:27
"So long, partner."
–Tom Hanks as Woody in *Toy Story 3* (2010)

INDEX OF MOVIES QUOTED

Michael Kent Winder, Sr. is the author of 14 published books, including the regional best-seller *Presidents & Prophets*. A lifelong fan of the movies, his first memory of cinema on the big screen was when his parents took him to see *The Empire Strikes Back* when he was a four-year-old. His favorite movie treat is frozen Junior Mints.

Mike holds an Honors BA in History and an MBA from the University of Utah, as well as a leadership certificate from Harvard's Kennedy School of Government. He was appointed by Governor Jon Huntsman to two terms on the Utah Board of State History and by Governor Gary Herbert to the Utah Museums Advisory Board.

Active in public affairs, Mike served four years as a West Valley City Councilman, four years as West Valley City Mayor, and six years as a legislator in the Utah House of Representatives. Today, Mike Winder is city manager of Millcreek, Utah, and involved with the boards of both Friends of Traditional Banking and St. Mark's Hospital.

Mike and his sweetheart Karyn just celebrated their 25th wedding anniversary. They are the proud parents of four: Jessica (married to Cory Lee), Michael, John, and Grace—the latter whom helped her dad as the research assistant for this book.